THE LORD'S NATION

DANIEL F. IRINEU

THE LORD'S NATION

Copyright © 2024 by Daniel F. Irineu
All rights reserved. No part of this book may be reproduced in any manner whatsoever without written permission except in the case of brief quotations embodied in critical articles and reviews.
First Printing, 2024
ISBN 978-65-01-21277-7
Learn more about the author at DanielFirineu.art.br

This book is dedicated to everyone who is in it, including my family, President and Sister Judd, and all of my companions.
Hope you enjoy it.

Contents

Dedication v
Text Insert ix

Introduction 1
1 A New Life Begins 3
2 The First Trial 11
3 São Paulo MTC Mission 23
4 A Missionary in the ICU 31
5 The Land of the Rising Sun 39
6 Inuyama 49
7 A New Mission President and a New Bike 59
8 Dangerous City 73
9 The Real Teacher 83
10 The First Typhoon 91
11 A New Companion 101
12 My First Thanksgiving 109
13 Lost at The Christmas Concert 117
14 Shougatsu 133
15 The Prophet Answers My Prayer 139
16 Fukuroi 145
17 We Help a Family to Move 155

18	An Apostle Visits My Mission	163
19	The Furnace of Affliction	173
20	After Much Tribulations Come The Blessings	181
21	Reaping Rice	187
22	Did You Hear the Angels?	195
23	It Wasn't a Waste of Time	203
24	COVID Strikes	211
25	Trapped in São Paulo	219
	Conclusion	229

About the Author   230

"As sorrowful, yet alway rejoicing; as poor, yet making many rich; as having nothing, and yet possessing all things."
2 Corinthians 6:10

Introduction

This book tells the story of my life as a missionary of The Church of Jesus Christ of Latter-Day Saints. As a member of the church, every healthy young man is invited to serve as a full-time missionary for two years. During these years, we preach and teach the gospel of Jesus Christ, and how He restored His Church these Latter-days. And that is what I did for two years in a land that I did not know and in a language that I knew nothing about it. That was the country of Japan.

My intention is to tell how my experience as a missionary was, from 2018 to 2020. I hope that if you are not a member of the church, you will learn a little more about our beliefs and about the missionaries. If you are a member of the church I want to share my testimony, through my experiences, that God really is our Heavenly Father and that he answers our prayers today. But first, I need to explain something about myself and give some context.

I was born in the South of Brazil, in the city of Passo Fundo. My parents are called Anna Paula and Domingos Irineu. I have two older siblings: Arthur and Susanna. Because of my father's work, we were always transferred around Brazil and we all were born in different states.

My parents were born in the Northeast, in the state of Pernambuco. My sister was born in Amazonas. Finally, my brother and I were born in the State of Rio Grande do Sul, in Passo Fundo.

When I was little, we moved again to a city Northeast of Brazil called João Pessoa. In 2011, when I was 12, we moved back to the South and started to live in the capital of Porto Alegre. After that, we never traveled because of my father's work again. Moving was never a big problem for me, because I was always very close to my family and my siblings were always my best friends.

My parents met the missionaries of the Church when they were teenagers and raised my siblings and I with the knowledge of the Gospel of Jesus Christ. We always went to church on Sundays and studied the Book of Mormon, The Bible, and other scriptures during the week.

Since very young, I knew that one day I would be a missionary for the Church of Jesus Christ of Latter-day Saints. However, faith is not something that we can borrow from others and it's definitely not something that we can inherit from our parents. I had to pray to know if the Church was true and I received a testimony from the Holy Ghost that it was indeed the restored Church of Jesus Christ.

Knowing that the church is true, I was certain that I needed to be a missionary, it was never a question to me. However, I prayed and studied the scriptures a lot to receive the desire to go on a mission because I knew that it wouldn't be easy to leave my family and friends for two ears.

The Lord blessed me with the desire to go and I did everything I needed to make myself ready to go on a mission. I sent my mission papers when I was 18 years old and waited with a mix of excitement and fear to know where I would serve as a missionary. The Lord would call me to go somewhere in the world, I knew that, and I was ready to serve anywhere.

But when the answer from the Church came, the papers that would tell me where I needed to go, told me that I had been called to serve in the Japan Nagoya Mission. I was beyond surprised. To be honest, I didn't even know where Nagoya was, though I had heard much about Tokyo in my life. I knew how to speak English, but didn't know any Japanese. Soon I realized that knowing English already was going to be a great blessing in my life as a missionary.

And here is where the story begins.

1

A New Life Begins

I always knew that saying goodbye to my family at the airport would be sad. I was very sad when my brother left to serve as a missionary, but this time, I was the one going away.

I hugged my family and friends who were at the airport with me and left to pass through the metal detectors. After I was in a different room, where people were waiting and getting in lines to board their planes, I realized that I had no idea where to go.

"What now?", I asked myself feeling suddenly worried. I had taken airplanes before, but usually, I had my parents to guide me. Gladly this problem was quickly solved, I approached an employee and showed my flight information. She told me where I needed to wait.

I was going to take a flight to São Paulo. There, I would stay in the Missionary Training Center (MTC) for 9 weeks. In the MTC, we learn about how to be a missionary and, in my case, to study Japanese, since I would need to know Japan's language to teach the gospel.

I sat close to the window of the plane and no one sat next to me. There were not many people in the airplane for some reason. The travel between Porto Alegre and São Paulo is very short by plane, less than 2 hours. I had so much in my head that I barely noticed the time and soon the plane was touching the ground again.

It was weird how I never asked much about the mission to my father or brother. I knew where they served and that they were preaching the gospel of Jesus Christ for two years. But I never asked about the specifics (or even thought about it).

What was the MTC like? How did everything work? Were there going to be a big group of missionaries like me in the airport?

I had no idea.

I left the airplane and got my baggage. Then, I left for the airport. I had never been to São Paulo, so everything in that city was also new to me. That was a man waiting for me as soon as I left. He was holding a square poster with the letters: CTM (MTC in Portuguese). I smiled and walked in his direction.

The man was dressed in a suit, like me, and told me that we still needed to wait for another missionary, and then we would go to the MTC. He was in a hurry, probably because he didn't want the other missionary to feel lost, not seeing anyone.

We quickly walked to another door and waited a little bit. The other missionary was a woman, Sister Vaz. She arrived and seemed to be as lost as me and that made me feel better.

I shook her hand and introduced myself.

— My name is Elder Irineu – I said with a smile. My name was Daniel França Irineu, but for the next two years, I would bear the title of "Elder" followed by my last name. Women were called "Sisters" followed by their last name.

We had nametags with our names and the name of the church, but the polite thing to do was to introduce ourselves.

Sister Vaz was nervous like me, but she was happy and easy to talk to.

— Where are you from? – She asked.

— Porto Alegre. And you?

— I'm from Minas Gerais – She answered.

— Cool! – I answered. I had never met anyone from that state, and that explained her accent, which I had never heard before.

My own accent was different from other Brazilians. Since I lived for a long time in the South and Northeast, my accent was a mixture of both and explained why everybody anywhere asked where I was from.

It turns out that Sister Vaz and I were the only missionaries arriving that morning, so we entered in a big black car and the man who greeted us drove us to the MTC. I always was a quiet person and talking to strangers was never one of my strengths, because of that, there was a lot of silence in the car.

The silence didn't bother me very much, because I always enjoyed car rides and looking at the view. But the driver probably was uneasy about the lack of conversations in the vehicle and started talking about the city and the places that we were seeing, almost like a tourist guide.

Sister Vaz was going to serve in Japan as well but on a different mission. She was going to the Japan Tokyo Mission. I was very excited to see the MTC because I had no idea what the building would look like. My brother failed to give me any good descriptions.

After some time, the driver parked inside the MTC and I saw the building for the first time. It was a very tall rectangular building. The walls were white, and it was surprisingly big. Some people greeted us, but the whole building looked empty. Apparently, it was past lunchtime and all the missionaries already were inside many classrooms.

Sister Vaz and I left our luggage in the hallway and entered a square room that was very pleasant. There was a table in the center, with two couches and two big chairs around it. A man brought us a sandwich and juice and said that unfortunately, that would have to be enough until dinner, but then we would eat as much as we wanted.

I wasn't really hungry. Everything was new and I was too nervous to eat. Sister Vaz and I started eating when suddenly someone entered the room. He was a man dressed the same way as me, but he looked happy and confident.

— Hello! How are you? – He asked with a big smile and shook my hand. Then did the same with Sister Vaz – How was your travel?

He looked so comfortable with the MTC that I imagined that he worked there. However, I took a better look at his suit and saw that he was a missionary just like me. Apparently, he just was much more outgoing and energetic about it. I smiled with my mistaken judgment.

The missionary's name was Elder Taneguti. He lived in São Paulo and because of that, he didn't need to take a flight to get there. His family drove him to the front door. It must have been nice. Definitely a different experience. He was going to serve on the Japan Kobe mission, the one on South from mine.

A man that actually worked there entered the room and explained that our companions would arrive today, but were not there yet. He and a Sister explained to us that we would take our luggage to our rooms and after would send emails to our families saying that we had arrived well.

They told us that there were only two elevators in the MTC and that missionaries were not allowed to use them.

— You are only going to use this elevator twice here – The man joked but was very sure of what was saying – Now and when you are leaving for the missionary field.

Unfortunately, his prediction was completely wrong.

My room was on the final floor of the MTC, the sixth floor, turning right from the stairs, and left from the elevator. The MTC was beautiful on the inside. Everything was clean and peaceful. It was like a giant church building, but it felt more like a temple, maybe because of the size.

Every hallway had many beautiful paintings related to Jesus Christ, the scriptures, and church history. Most paintings I had never seen before. I went to my room and saw a big rectangular room with three big bunk beds. Those bunk beds were made of wood and were really high.

Two bunk beds were close to the wall on the right and the middle one was next to the wall on the left. In front of each buck bed, there were two closets and a small table with a chair, a perfect place to sit down and write a little.

On the wall in front of the door, at the end of the room, there was an enormous window that showed the big blue sky and a great view of São Paulo. I chose the bunk bed closest to the window and farther from the door. Elder Taneguti took the bunk bed in the middle of the room.

I placed my backpack on the bottom bed. I already slept on a buck bed back home and my brother always had the one at the top, so I was used to that. My companion probably wouldn't have a problem with that either, people usually rather stay on the top one. But, honestly, that bunk bed was so high that I was afraid to fall in the middle of that night and get injured.

After that, we went to the second floor, using the big stairs that we should gotten used to using. On the second floor, there were rooms with computers that we would use to communicate with our family. In that room, there were other missionaries, including Elder Cavalcanti. A short man that seemed to be as quiet as me.

He was Elder Taneguti's companion, and they both hugged when met. There were other sisters there as well. Later I would learn that they were Sister Rebouças, Galdino, Torres, and Mello.

— You can use your new missionary email to send emails to your family. Please tell them that you have arrived safely – The employee told us.

"That might be a problem", I thought. I was not completely sure of my family's email. Why would I? I never really sent emails to them, but it would be easy using my regular email. With the new one, their contacts wouldn't be saved.

I opened my email and was very happy to see that every member of my family had already sent me emails. That was a great relief, this way I only needed to answer their messages.

I told them that the trip was great and everything was ok. We talked for a few minutes and I explained that we would only be able to talk again, using emails, on Preparation Day (Missionaries have one day to take care of personal affairs and that is the day they talk with their friends, and family. This day is usually called P-day).

After my time to talk with them finished, another Elder entered the room. He was wearing a blue suit and was a little taller than me. His name was Elder Orsi, my companion for the next 9 weeks.

We hugged each other and introduced ourselves. I had seen him before, on an Instagram page where people posted their pictures and the place they were called to serve. He was called to the Japan Nagoya Mission, same as me, maybe that's why I remembered him. Later we all mentioned that most of us had seen each other on similar pages on Instagram.

I didn't talk much to him while he was talking with his family, because I knew he didn't have much time to talk to them. When his time was up, I showed him our room and he chose the bed above mine.

For some reason, we all chose the same bunk beds as our companions. Maybe we all thought it was necessary, but it really wasn't. Other two missionaries arrived that day, Elder Abreu and Elder Santos. We all, that had arrived that day, would serve in Japan and all the Elders would stay in the same room.

Also, we were part of the same "district", which meant we would do pretty much everything together. We would learn Japanese in the same classes, have the same instructors, and have the same time to eat and do other activities. That first day, the MTC gave us many materials that we would use to study the scriptures and, mainly, Japanese. They also gave us a padlock to use in our closets, if we felt like it. But no one in my room used the padlocks, myself included.

That was how my mission started. Most people don't stay long in the MTC, but some people that are going to learn specific languages (like Japanese), stay the longest, 9 weeks (9 weeks is the longest missionaries can stay in the São Paulo MTC). That night I said a prayer before sleeping and thanked for everything working out in the end. There was no reason to be as nervous as I was during that day. But I suppose it is inevitable to feel nervous when you start a completely new adventure where the future is unknown.

2

The First Trial

Before going on my mission, I had made a goal: I would write in my journal every single day, writing the city where I was and the day of my mission. My first night on the MTC I wrote about my first day before sleeping, but not with many details since I was tired and needed to sleep.

On the second day, it was weird to wake up at the MTC. For a second, I thought I would wake up at my house and everything was different. Gladly, the MTC is very good at keeping missionaries busy. Almost every single hour of our day was panned and delivered to us. Because of that, I didn't have any time to miss my family or my old routine.

The MTC had hundreds of missionaries from everywhere in Brazil, and people from other countries, like Argentina, Chile, Uruguai, United States, and even people from other continents, like Africa. Not one of them would stay as long as us in the MTC, but the missionaries from the United States would stay there for 6 weeks, three weeks less than us.

All of the missionaries were divided into groups called "districts", each district had a classroom where the district spent most of the time, studying the gospel and the new language. My district was the Japanese district, all of us would fly together to Japan, but to different missions. The ones going to Nagoya with me were: My companion, Elder Orsi, Sister Galdino, and Elder Cavalcanti.

And many districts together were a "Zone". Each district had a "district leader" and each zone had "zone leaders". I learned that that was exactly how the missionaries were divided outside of the MTC, so it was good practice for us to learn.

The MTC had a very good feeling about it. It was the Spirit of the Lord, the Holy Ghost. It was almost impossible not to feel good at that place and I quickly imagined why, hundreds of people were there studying the scriptures, praying, and sharing their testimonies about the Lord Jesus Christ and the scriptures. It was impossible not to feel the Holy Ghost.

We had many classes about the mission field and met our instructors, Sister Uchiyama and Sister Medeiros. They both had served their missions in Japan and would teach us the language and how to be as missionaries.

I soon learned what it really meant to be a missionary. Of course, my purpose was to share the gospel of Jesus Christ and baptize converts, but being a missionary also meant being a representative of Jesus Christ. It meant being honest with everyone and with the Lord, truly caring about other people, and being willing to help at any moment.

That day, we needed to check something on our church accounts as missionaries. My hole district went to one of the rooms filled with computers and another MTC instructor, Brother Siqueira, helped us to set up our accounts. He came to me and asked:

— What is your name?

— Daniel – I answered automatically.

He looked at me with an annoyed expression for some reason. It took me a few seconds to realize what was his problem.

— Elder Irineu – I corrected and laughed a little bit. Elder Orsi also laughed, but not the instructor – I need to get used to that.

It really took us some time. On the first few days, we would all say our first names and quickly correct ourselves.

On our third day, we started to learn Japanese. Sister Uchiyama was very strict as she helped us to establish goals, and encouraged us to practice as much as possible. She always spoke Japanese at the classroom and mostly we had no idea what she was saying. She also wanted us to do "SYL" (Speak Your Language) as much as possible, which meant that she wanted us only to speak Japanese with each other.

That was more achievable with the American missionaries coming to Brazil because everybody spoke Portuguese and the other people from their country were learning Portuguese as well. However, we were the only ones learning Japanese in the entire MTC, so the only ones who could talk to us in that language were the instructors.

But we all did our best. All of us were writing new words, memorizing sentences, and learning Hiragana and Katakana, the first two alphabets in the Japanese language. There is a third one, Kanji, but Kanji has many thousands of "letters", so we decided to worry about Kanji after fully memorizing Hiragana and Katakana.

I had taken classes of Japanese after learning that I would go to Nagoya, and because of that I already knew Hiragana and Katakana. That helped, but I still needed to learn vocabulary and grammar. On that same day, Sister Uchiyama told us that we would all teach a lesson in Japanese that same night.

— What?! – We all asked – But we don't know Japanese, how are we going to teach a lesson?

— You are only going to learn by practicing and asking the Lord for help – Sister Uchiyama answered with no hesitation.

Elder Orsi and I prepared the best way we could. We searched our books for short sentences about the gospel. Those books had many sentences that explained key doctrines of the gospel and the Church. One section was dedicated to teaching us how to pray in Japanese.

We selected some sentences and prepared our message the best way we could. A companionship at a time, we walked to the stairs went to the second floor, and knocked at the door where Sister Uchiyama was waiting for us. She pretended to be someone from Japan that didn't know the Church and we needed to teach her.

The classroom was designed to be Japanese. There were many Eastern objects decorating the place, a very small squared table in the middle, and cushions for us to kneel in. We need to teach the entire class on our knees (this position is called "seiza" in Japanese and it is a formal and respectful way to sit at someone's house). At first, it was hard to teach a lesson of 40 minutes on our knees, but we were far more worried about teaching in Japanese.

We taught by reading the Japanese sentences and even invited her to say the final prayer. Sister Uchiyama never made things easy for us and pretended to be a very close-hearted person. She also had no problem in saying that she didn't understand what we were trying to say.

By the end of the lesson, I was very happy. I didn't know any Japanese but felt the Lord's help. We were able to teach the gospel in another language and I even invited her to pray. To me, it was impossible to deny that the Lord was helping us. He definitely helped me that night.

Unfortunately, the other missionaries didn't feel so well. They were crushed since they couldn't speak the language and say what they wanted to say. Everybody was very visibly sad.

— But we did it! – I said excitedly.

— Elder, we can't speak Japanese! – Elder Orsi said very upset.

— Did you think we could? – I asked with good humor.

He did not think that question was funny.

— Don't be sad – I said to him and to the other two Elders: Abreu and Santos – Of course we cannot speak Japanese right now, but we will learn!

But my attempts to improve everyone's mood failed. The Elders were all sad and many of them cried. I, however, was very grateful for the Lord's help. Not that I had good Japanese at that moment, I didn't.

But I saw no reason to be so sad, we would all learn, and the Lord would help us.

The next day was similar, we were all very busy, and the MTC was full of rules, just like any mission. Missionaries need to obey many rules about how to conduct themselves, the time to sleep and wake up, and never be alone. None of the rules ever really bothered me, but we did have one problem in our room. None of us had an alarm to wake us at the right time.

I went to the MTC sure that someone else would have an alarm, and so did every single Elder in my room. That was a problem because we needed to be up at 6:30 am. Elder Orsi showed us that he actually had a very modern clock, it was a beautiful white square with the digital time on it.

The only problem is that it made no noise. At 6:30 it made such a faint sound that Elder Orsi needed to sleep with the clock right next to his ear. After the clock woke him, he would jump out of bed and turn on the lights, waking us. It just didn't work one day and a man who worked in the MTC opened our door very angry and said:

— Elders, if you don't wake up, the MTC president will have a word with you.

We all jumped and looked at Elder Orsi, who said that he really didn't hear the alarm. I didn't blame him, none of us did. That alarm was so weak that it wouldn't wake up any of us.

But everything was going well and everyone in my district was getting along really well. Elder Orsi was very funny and was always cracking up a joke, that was something I was grateful for. In matter of fact, my whole district was very funny, we were always laughing during breakfast, Lunch, and dinner. That made it easier for all of us to adapt to our new life as missionaries.

One of the Sisters was called Rebouças, she was very tall and excited about everything. She was not shy, at all, and would scream at random moments "I LOVE YOU" to any elder or sister close to her.

At first, we thought it was funny and a little weird, but soon anyone would scream the same to her in response.

But probation always comes. It is one of the ways that the Lord uses to teach us to have faith and patience. After five days, my left knee started to hurt and the pain only grew with a strange feeling on it, as if it was swollen on the inside. I knew it wasn't normal and started to get really worried.

I knew that the stairs were not helping. My room was on the last floor and we needed to go up and down many times in a single day, every day. Eventually, I went to the doctor and, on P-day, I asked my family what I should do since it was getting worse.

Basically, the stairs on the MTC were hurting me, it caused this problem. Many people believe that stairs are good for the knees, which unfortunately is not true. The MTC doctor was a very serious man and didn't talk much, but asked me to buy a knee brace.

Elder Orsi and I left the MTC, crossed the street, and went to a pharmacy. There, I bought the knee brace. Elder Orsi was very quiet about the subject, probably worried about me. And most people in the MTC didn't help much, they all said that this injury would be a serious problem, and it could make me go back home. This thought was beyond stressful to me. I was terrified by this idea.

Gladly, my parents decided to help. They called the MTC and apparently talked with many people, including the President of the MTC. But I didn't know that at that moment.

The same day that I bought the knee bracelet, at night, I went to the Help Desk with Elder Orsi to ask for some ice for my knee. There, I met a woman called Sister Tamires. I never had seen her during the day. She had short hair, a beautiful smile, and was extremely kind.

I told her my situation and she was the first person in the MTC, that day, who was very optimistic about my problem. Of course, Elder Orsi was also very supportive, but talking to Sister Tamires made me feel so much better.

— Don't worry, Elder Irineu. Missionaries have problems with the knees sometimes, but everything will be fine – She said with naturality – You should come every night and get ice with me.

— Really? – I asked.

— Of course! I also have a spray for contusions and a missionary health guide for you – She said and immediately started looking for all of the materials in her office.

Elder Orsi and I went to the stairs after that and walked back to our room on the last floor. Sister Tamires, to me, was an example of how missionaries and members of the church should be, someone willing to help, with an optimistic attitude.

The following day, the president of the MTC asked to talk to me. His name was President Martins Silva. He was an inspired man, someone who clearly had a great knowledge of the gospel. His face seemed very serious, so, many missionaries had the first impression that he was someone angry. But after he started talking you could see that he was a great church leader, with a surprisingly great sense of humor. I had never seen him being unpleasant with anyone, even though he was firm when he needed to be.

On my first Sunday in the MTC, he gave a talk to all missionaries and spoke with a great Spirit. After that talk, I always hoped that he would speak again in any devotional or sacrament meeting.

Still, when he called my companion and me, I got very nervous. Elder Orsi and I entered his office and looked around. His office was a rectangle with a window on the left side. On the right side, there was a painting of the atonement of Jesus Christ on Getsemani. I set on the left chair, in front of the President.

— Elder Irineu, why didn't you tell me that you couldn't use the stairs? – He asked calmly.

I didn't have a quick answer. I didn't know that he knew about my knee.

— I didn't know it would be so bad for my knee – I answered with sincerity.

— I talked to your parents and they explained the situation to me – He continued – If you can't use the stairs, you will use the elevator. There is no problem. I would do this for any missionary because my purpose here is to help prepare you for your mission. So, it is a big problem if you hurt yourself because of the MTC – He added with a good sense of humor.

Elder Orsi and I laughed. I was relieved he wasn't angry with me, and I think my companion was also very relieved.

— You are still going to stay here for a long time, which is good because it will give you time to heal. But it also means that you will need authorization to use the elevator – The President continued – I laminated it because a simple piece of paper would be destroyed in the next eight weeks.

— Thank you so much, President – I said feeling really grateful.

— No problem. But if you have any other problem, please talk to me – He answered with a smile.

After we left his office, we walked toward the elevator to go back to our classroom.

— See you soon – Elder Orsi said while turning to the stairs.

— Where are you going? – I asked. As companions, we shouldn't leave each other's side.

— To use the stairs – Elder Orsi answered.

— You are going to use the elevator with me – I said.

— I don't have an authorization to use it.

— Of course you have! You are my companion. So, if I can use the elevator, so can you – I said.

— I don't know… - Elder Orsi wasn't sure. I understood his fear since the prohibition to use the elevator was surprisingly strict.

— Let's ask the President – I said.

We came back to his office and asked if Elder Orsi would also use the elevator with me.

— Of course! – He answered – You are companions, so you both can use the elevator.

I did receive an authorization to use the elevator and always carried it with me in my pocket. It was funny how people always got angry about me using the elevator. Many MTC instructors started to reprimand us when saw us using the elevator, then I showed my authorization and explained that I needed to use it because of my knee. Some of them accepted well, others still seemed to be bothered. Other missionaries also looked a little annoyed with us using the elevator.

After that, my knee stopped getting worse. But many people would always make comments such as "Are you sure you can go on a mission?" or "If your knee is bad right now, don't you think it will be worse on a mission?"

I think most people were worried and didn't have bad intentions by asking these questions, but it was something that I always carried on my mind. My greatest fear at that moment. My answer to these people where always: "It will be fine." Or "I'm sure I will be OK."

Even Elder Orsi would step in sometimes and say: "He will be fine! Don't listen to them, Elder Irineu." He was a very good friend.

One day, Orsi asked me if I was worried about my knee being a problem during my mission. I gave him my honest answer:

— I will not go home because of my knee. Not even if it cost me my leg!

Maybe I was being dramatic, but it was exactly what I felt. I was determined to face this challenge. Later that night, I asked Elder Orsi to give me a priesthood blessing. He did give me a blessing from the priesthood so I could be healed. During the blessing, I felt everything would work out for the best and I didn't need to go to any doctor anymore. I really felt my knee would be fine.

One night I noticed that my left knee had some red dots on it. My brother always was very allergic to many things, so I immediately noticed it to be an allergy. It should be because of the knee brace, so I stopped using for that afternoon and night.

The next day my allergy was much worse. But it was P-day and we needed to go very early to have our breakfast and then go to the São Paulo temple. I loved going to the temple, the House of the Lord, and the São Paulo temple is special for many reasons. It is the first temple in South America and it is the temple where my parents got sealed for all eternity.

But, after we came back from the temple, after lunch, I knew that my knee was worse. It was itching so much that it made me crazy. The doctor was not in the MTC that day for some reason, so one of the missionary couples (Elder and Sister Whitiker) gave me an antiallergic cream to pass on my knee.

The next day, my knee was worse. It was completely swollen and very red. I went to the doctor and he gave me a different cream and some medicine. This time, it worked. The itching stopped and at the end of the day, it had come back to a normal size.

Sometimes, during class, I would start itching my knee, and Elder Orsi would hit my hand and say:

— Stop Irineu! It will get worse!

That always made me laugh. He was very observant. After my knee came back to its normal size, the bright red started to fade and my skin became very dry. That made my knee and a part of my leg change color for a while. At night, Other Elders would see my leg and become very worried.

— Are you ok? Is that a skin disease?

— It's nothing. Just an allergy – I answered. The allergy problem actually didn't make me nervous at all.

After some time, my knee came back to normal and I only had the regular pain that didn't go away for a long time. But it was fine. I felt in my heart that I didn't need to worry. Also, I could deal with the pain. After I stopped using the stairs, it stopped hurting that much.

I wasn't the only victim of those stairs. One Elder, some time later actually faced a much worse problem. He missed a step and hurt the ligaments of his heel. He had to be taken to the hospital and had his foot immobilized. He started using crunches after that for the whole time I had left in the MTC. Other missionaries in my district also started having knee pains, but that was much later.

My whole district was worried about me and they all fastened and prayed so that I would be completely cured. That touched me deep in my heart. It is amazing to feel the love of so many people who care about you. That was another example of great missionaries to me. All of them of my district.

3

São Paulo MTC Mission

On our first P-day in the MTC, we left the building to buy an alarm for us. There was a specific distance that all missionaries could go outside the MTC building and everything we needed was there. All the Elders gave in some money, and we bought a big, red, classic clock. It was red and had a bell on top that would make a lot of noise every morning. Exactly what we wanted.

I loved the clock for some reason and named it "Mormon", my favorite prophet. The next day, we decided to have a little fun. We all woke up earlier in the morning and left the room to get ready for the day. We made sure to close the door after us and leave the lights out.

The same MTC employee who wasn't very nice, opened the door and said angrily:

— Elders!

But when he turned on the lights, there was no one in the room. I was the only one going back to the room, so the other Elders didn't see any of this.

— Hello brother, good morning – I said with a smile and entered the room.

He looked very confused but answered:

— Good morning.

I do understand why some MTC employees could be rude sometimes. Many missionaries can be very reckless and break the rules for any reason. Even worse, they will break rules for no reason and create serious problems for themselves. So, it is necessary to be strict with most rules. This brother couldn't know for sure that we were telling the truth about not having a good alarm. But after we bought our clock "Mormon", we never had a problem with waking up again.

The days followed in the MTC very quickly and I got used to the routine. It was weird because time was flying, but at the same time, it seemed that I was there for many months.

One morning, Elder Abreu woke up with conjunctivitis. His eyes were very red and we were all impressed. How did he get conjunctivitis? He was the only one in the MTC with it. Elder Orsi found the whole situation very funny.

— Hey, Irineu, that is a beautiful tie you are wearing today – Orsi said out loud while we were all studying the scriptures in our classroom.

— Thank you – I was waiting for the joke.

— It's the same color as Abreu's eyes!

My tie was a very bright red. We all laughed a lot, including Elder Abreu. Orsi made many other jokes that morning, like:

— Abreu seems furious, his eyes are turning red!

In the afternoon, Sister Uchiyama entered the room saying "konichiwa!" with a big smile. We all answered and got ready to try to understand the class in Japanese (usually we couldn't, but we did learn new words with her every day).

She looked at Elder Abreu and immediately got curious.

— What happened to your eyes?

— We think it is conjunctivitis – We all answered.

Sister Uchiyama nodded with her head and left the room. We all looked at each other for a few seconds and she immediately came back with hand sanitizer for all of us.

Sister Uchiyama said that Elder Abreu needed to go to the doctor and treat his eyes. She was right, of course, but Elder Abreu did not want to miss any lesson. He was convinced after some time and went to the doctor with Elder Santos, his companion.

Unfortunately, Elder Abreu needed to stay in his room until he got better. It would be a problem if all the missionaries in the MTC got infected with him, so it was for safety. This made Elder Abreu very sad and we all felt bad for him. Being stuck in a room alone the whole day with nothing to do other than reading the scriptures and trying to learn Japanese alone, was very boring.

The season was also changing and some of us got a cold. I only lost my voice, but Sister Rebouças was the next one visiting the doctor. Maybe going to the doctor was a necessary experience for all of us in the MTC.

Elder Cavalcanti said it was very unfair for me to lose my voice:

— Irineu, you are the quiet one of all of us. Why are YOU the one who lost your voice? – He asked almost angrily.

— No idea – I answered with a very weak voice.

On the third day without having a voice, Sister Mello came to say something:

— Irineu, did you know that honey is very good for our throats?

Sister Mello was a very funny sister with short curly hair. She was usually nice to everyone and Elder Orsi used to call her "Emma Smith" because of her hair.

— Really? – I had no idea.

— Yes! I think you should drink some honey.

— Where am I going to get honey in the MTC? – I asked – Maybe I can look at the grocery store on P-day...

— I have honey! – She said.

— You do?

— Yes. It is very good for your hair – She informed me.

I also had no idea honey was good for our hair. She brought me honey later that day and I drank some of it.

— Thank you! You're awesome! – I told her.

And she was completely correct, my throat came back to normal after that.

But not everything was flowers. I was blessed to get along well with my companion, but some other companionships had more difficulty with their relationships. Elder Taneguti and Elder Cavalcanti had some problems getting along. They used to fight very often and the rest of us ignored them most of the time, trying to give them some privacy.

I thought they would eventually overcome any problems, but the situation got worse and worse. The problem between them escalated to the point that we heard that the President would rearrange the companionships.

Elder Orsi and I were very worried about that. We were already very used to each other and didn't want to change companions. We were already with so much to do, trying to learn how to teach the gospel, be good missionaries, and Japanese. Changing companions would make everything more complicated. Also, we got along very well with each other, maybe we wouldn't be so lucky with other people.

All the Elders were called to the office of President Martins Silva. All six of us were standing and the President picked up a small piece of paper from his table.

— It's not common for us to change companionships during the MTC, but I have here the new arrangements... — He started saying.

Elder Orsin looked at me terrified. I probably had the same expression.

— President, wait! – Elder Cavalcanti suddenly said.

He stopped talking, surprised.

— Elder Taneguti and I talked a lot and we decided to stay together. We will work things out – He explained.

— Are you sure? – The President looked to Taneguti.

— Yes – Elder Taneguti said – We want to stay together.

The President smiled. Maybe he was happy with their decision, but it was hard to say, he was someone happy and smiled at us at any moment.

— I have the new arrangements right here. So you need to be certain – He warned.

— We are – They both said.

— That's great! – The President said happy.

We left his office and Elder Santos hugged Elder Abreu at the same time Elder Orsi hugged me. We were all very relieved.

— Common, it wouldn't be that bad to be our companions! – Elder Cavalcanti joked to us.

— Of course not! – I said. I was not lying, but I also didn't want to change companions.

One day, Sister Mello was not feeling well and asked me for a priesthood blessing. I was very honored with her request and said a small prayer, asking the Lord to help me. In the missionary handbook, there were instructions on how to perform priesthood ordinances, so I knew how to do it, but it was the first time I gave a priesthood blessing. I felt the Spirit very strongly and she felt much better after the blessing and for the rest of the day.

The sisters were also having some problems. Siter Mello, Vaz, and Torres were a trio, and they often had long private conversations to get along better. They set goals and established rules among each other. It worked very well, I think.

As the weeks passed, many missionaries left for the mission field and many others arrived, but we were always there. The missionaries coming from the United States stayed for 6 weeks, but even they left before us. Twice our district was the only one in the MTC for a day. That made us say that we were already serving on an unexpected mission, the "São Paulo MTC Mission".

However, I do think that this long time in the MTC helped me to adapt to the mission. I did miss my family, but it would have been worse if I had gone straight to Japan. Definitely.

During this time I learned much about the Holy Ghost and our Savior. One day, Sister Uchiyama taught us something important:

— It's not hard because it is in Japanese.

— Yes, it is – We all answered.

— No. If I asked you to teach me about the Restoration right now, how would you do it? – She asked one of us – How would you approach me?

— In Portuguese?

— Yes – She answered.

We were all in silence for a few seconds.

— If you don't know what to say in Portuguese, you will not know in any language – Sister Uchiyama explained – Teaching the gospel is something that requires preparation, that is why in your personal studies, you need to focus on the lesson and on the people you are teaching. This way, the Spirit will remind you of what you already know.

Sister Medeiros also taught us a lot about the Spirit:

— The one who really teaches anyone is the Holy Ghost. The Lord uses us as instruments on His hand, but the one who will touch other's hearts is the Spirit of the Lord – Sister Medeiros said – You don't need to speak in perfect Japanese, but if you are honest, sincere, and speak with your heart, the Spirit will touch others. It doesn't matter how simple is your sentence.

President Martins Silva would talk to us every once in a while. He would come to our class and ask us how we were doing. He was always very pleasant and every missionary in our district loved him.

There was also a missionary couple in the MTC, Elder and Siter Whitaker. They helped the MTC President a lot in many things. Elder Whitaker had served in Brazil when he was young, so he knew Portuguese very well. Sister Whitaker had more difficulty with our language, but she was the one in charge of the MTC choir (all the missionaries sang in the choir).

My district loved to sing. We sang hymns going to the temple, and in Japanese before our classes to practice. We asked Sister Whitiker if we could sing "Peace in Christ" in Japanese during a devotional. She loved the idea and made us very excited about it.

We would practice the hymn every day before going to our rooms. Elder Taneguti played the piano for us. He played very well and the instrumental for this song was beautiful.

The whole MTC sang the arrangement we created and we sang alone the final part in Japanese, with Elder Taneguti playing the piano. The lyrics of the song are beautiful and say that we can always have Peace in the Lord, even when we can't have peace in the world. The Spirit was very strong during that song and everyone cried, feeling the Savior's love.

During that time in the MTC, I read a scripture that said: " But behold, there shall be many—at that day when I shall proceed to do a marvelous work among them, that I may remember my covenants which I have made unto the children of men, that I may set my hand again the second time to recover my people, which are of the house of Israel." (2 Nephi 29:1 – Book of Mormon)

It is very common in the scriptures to read this term, "a marvelous work". And I realized that, at that moment, I was a part of this marvelous work, I was a missionary called to serve and preach the gospel. Not only me but hundreds of people around the MTC and the world. We were all from different cultures, places, and Nations, but were all together, united through the gospel of Jesus Christ, preaching the gospel to many other people and nations.

4

A Missionary in the ICU

While I was in the MTC, I had my birthday. On May 28th, I turned 19 years old. When the day was coming, I wondered if it would be a good day, since I always used to do something with my family, and now that wouldn't be possible. But the Lord blessed me very much and, on my birthday, a member of the Quorum of the Twelve Apostles, Elder Cook, came to the MTC.

I was called to say the first prayer of the devotional and every single missionary shook hands with Elder and Sister Cook. I was impressed by how Sister Cook was kind and how she spook with the Spirit. I also felt a very strong testimony that Elder Cook was an Apostle of the Lord, he spoke beautiful things and encouraged us to seek guidance through the Holy Ghost and write down the personal revelations that the Lord gives us.

My family also sent me a package with two new knee braces (that were made of a material for allergic people) and some normal medicaments for pain and allergy, just in case. All of those gifts were very useful for the next months of my mission. As a matter of fact, I used one of those knee braces for the rest of my mission, it never gave me any allergy.

It's a good thing I was doing a great job writing on my journal every day. President Martins Silva called Elder Orsi and me as zone leaders and "zone leaders of the zone leaders" that would be the equivalent of Mission President Assistants. That gave me the opportunity to serve others more. I also learned that serving was the best way of spending my days and a learned more while serving.

The weeks passed and we were all very excited to leave on our missions. But the stairs started making more victims. Elder Cavalcanti also started to feel pain in his knees, had to go to the doctor, and had many medical exams. Elder Santos started to have pains, as well.

Gladly we would serve in Japan with bikes, and that is very good for the knees, since it does not have an impact. One day, Sister Vaz started to feel pains in her leg and asked me for a priesthood blessing. I could understand very well the affliction of feeling pains as they were felling. I gave her a blessing and felt the Spirit of the Lord very strongly as I spoke. Later that night, Sister Vaz told me that she was feeling great and didn't feel any pain anymore. I was very grateful for the Lord's blessing.

One day, we learned about something serious that were happening with an Elder of the MTC. Elder Mcarty, who had just arrived in Brazil, had gone to the hospital because the left side of his body was swallowing, a condition called "Thrombosis". At the hospital, they discovered that this was happening because he had a deformity in one of his ribs.

Elder McCarty had to stay in the hospital because of all these problems. But, since he was a missionary, he needed to have a companion with him always and he didn't know any Portuguese yet, so it had to be a missionary that could translate for him at the hospital.

Because of that, my district was chosen to spend time with him, since almost all of us knew English. One companionship would go to the hospital, one of us would stay with him and the other would comeback with the other missionary.

Knowing English was actually very important for us because all of the material that we had to study Japanese was written in English. I was actually surprised with my English when I arrived at the MTC.

I knew that I could watch movies and TV shows in English without subtitles, but it was in the MTC that I noticed that I could have long conversations in English and had no problem hearing church talks or conferences in English.

Unfortunately, Elder McCarty's situation wasn't simple. The doctors explained to him that he would need to have surgery and remove his rib. Because of this, he went to the ICU.

I couldn't spend the night with him in the ICU because the Elder that stayed there would have to sleep in a tiny, simple chair and I had scoliosis. Sleeping a whole night in the chair would cause me a lot of pain for the next few days. Because of that, Elder Whitaker told me that I couldn't go, but Elder Orsi could.

We went to the hospital, one of the best hospitals of São Paulo, and Elder Orsi stayed there. I met Elder Mcarty and talked to him for a little while. It was impressive how calm he was. In his situation I would be very afraid, being alone and needing surgery in a new country. Walking around in the ICU also made me very grateful for my own health as I saw many people in difficult situations.

I came back to the MTC with Elder Taneguti and was companion with him and Elder Cavalcanti or Elder Santos and Abreu, since I also couldn't be alone. This kept happening for some days. Until Elder Orsi and I asked if we couldn't place more missionaries to go as well, this way it wouldn't be only the four of us. The MTC had hundreds of missionaries, there were definitely more people that could speak English and Portuguese.

Elder Whitaker said that if we could find more Elders, we could explain the situation to them and ask them to be put on the list. So, the both of us got a piece of paper and started walking around in the MTC, knocking on doors and asking if there were Elders in that district that could speak English. We talked with one room and wrote the names of two Elders.

We walked toward the next room and knocked. An instructor opened the door.

— Excuse me, we need to ask the missionaries if they can speak English, so they can stay with Elder Mcarty, who is in the hospital... —We started explaining.

— No Elders! – The instructor quickly interrupted – We are learning important things here and you are wasting our time.

We were shocked by his attitude. But someone quickly appeared next to us.

— What is happening here? – Sister Uchiyama asked very seriously.

— Your missionaries were interrupting my class... —The man started saying.

— No. I believe they were asking if the missionaries could help another Elder who is in need – She said firmly.

— They would need to stay a whole day with the other missionary, and that would make them lose over a day of learning – The other instructor argued.

— And that is exactly what had been happening with every Elder in my district for the last week – Sister Uchiyama responded – Is there someone here who can speak English?

One Elder raised his hand.

— Elder, please talk to Elder Whitaker and give him your name – She asked.

— I will do that – He answered. It seemed he wanted to help.

— Thank you – Sister Uchiyama said and closed the door. She turned to us – Why are the two of you doing this? It should be an instructor doing this, it will be far more effective.

— Well, we asked Elder Whitaker if we could find more people... – I started explaining.

— Give me the list, and I will find someone to take care of this. And you two should be on class – She said to us while taking the list from Elder Orsi's hand.

That was one of the reasons why we liked Sister Uchiyama so much.

More Elders were added to the list that could visited Elder Mcarty and that was very good for our district. It was our last week on the MTC and our planning became very confusing. Some changes were happening at the MTC, and there were problems with our hours. Because of that, we didn't have time to do laundry or even packing for our trip.

I and the other missionaries going to the Japan Nagoya Mission received a letter from our Mission President, his name was Ishiii. In his letter to me, he told me that I would need to have a bag to spend the first two days in the field and the rest of my things would be sent to my first area. He also asked me to spend my time on the plane the same way prophets in the scriptures would. I shouldn't watch movies or this kind of thing.

This wasn't a problem, I thought. I loved to read, write, and study the scriptures, so I decided to take the book "Jesus, The Christ" with me. It was a deep and fascinating book written by James E. Talmage, that I had started reading at the MTC.

One day, on our final week, all the missionaries were packing. In our first week, all of them had taken all of their clothes out and placed on the wardrobes. I didn't do that because I didn't want the trouble of needing to pack again to leave the MTC. I had used only the necessary for the MTC. I suggested this to the other Elders, but none of them followed my advice.

Because of this, I sat on one of the chairs and watched all of them packing as fast as they could. The idea of finally going to Japan made me very happy and excited. I couldn't wait to put everything I learned at the MTC into practice.

— Did you guys realized that by this time next week we are going to be in another country? In a place that we don't know, in a city that we never heard about, with someone that we never met?! – I said with a big smile.

— Why are you doing this?! – Elder Cavalcanti asked terrified – Are you trying to make me cry?!

I laughed a lot. I suppose it was also a scary thought.

— Sorry – I said.

But leaving was also sad. We had become friends with so many people in the MTC, and now we would never see them again. On Sunday we would leave to the airport, but there were two groups. Me, Orsi, Cavalcanti, Sister Galdino, and Sister Rebouças would go together in the afternoon and fly together to Nagoya. That was the final destination for most of us, but Sister Rebouças would take another plane there and go to Sapporo, her mission. The others would go later that night.

The van that was supposed to take us to the airport was late, so we were all talking for a while. We commented on how we all met and Sister Vaz said:

— Elder Irineu talks a lot now, but coming here he didn't say a word. The ride on the car was so silent. The driver even started talking – She commented laughing.

— You could have said something! – I said in my defense.

— I couldn't think of anything! – She said.

We all laughed and after some time a big van arrived and the driver was in a lot of hurry. Of course, he was late. He came to us and started helping us to put all of our luggage on the van, then he said:

— Now you need to give me the padlocks and we can go.

— What padlocks? – We all asked.

— The ones you received on your first day! – He said as if it were obvious.

Maybe it should be. But no one told us we would need to give back any padlocks.

— You need to give them to me so we can go! – He said seriously.

Maybe the padlocks weren't a problem for missionaries that were in the MTC for a few weeks, but we were there for over two months, that is more than an entire transfer in the missionary field.

We all started looking for our padlocks. The sister looked at their bags and the rest of us went back to our rooms on the sixth floor.

Everybody found the padlocks, except for me. I couldn't find mine anywhere. I couldn't even remember where I put it on the first day.

So, I had an idea. I took Elder Abreu's padlock and went to Elder Taneguti, who was close to me.

— Taneguti, I am going to give this padlock as my own. After we leave, you need to find Elder Abreu and explain that I took his. You can go to the help desk and explain the situation to the MTC, they will give another padlock to Abreu – I explained.

— I will do this. Don't worry – Taneguti said calmly.

And that is what I did. Maybe it wasn't right, but it was the best solution at the moment. Later I apologized to Abreu and he told me that everything was fine and I shouldn't worry about it.

So, we entered the van and he drove us to the airport. I never imagined, when I arrived at the MTC, that it would be so sad leaving it. But it was. Now I was going to Japan and my work as a full-time missionary would finally start.

5

The Land of the Rising Sun

My travel was very long, and I was very grateful that I wasn't alone. My first flight left at night from São Paulo and it would take eleven hours to arrive at Frankfurt, Germany.

I sat between two people, a woman on my left side and a man on my right side. I had a good conversation with the man and told him about the church and that I was a missionary. The woman only knew how to speak Spanish, so I couldn't talk to her very much. But she slept for the entire trip anyways (I was very impressed with her ability to sleep so well on the airplane). I always find it very hard to sleep in the airplane, not sure why.

I focused on my Mission President's request not to watch any movies and wrote on my journal (it was day 62 of my mission), and read "Jesus, The Christ". Unfortunately, it was almost impossible not to see the screen of the person in front of me. I did pay attention to see the movies he would choose and was nervous when he almost chose a movie that I really liked. Gladly, he chose a movie that I hated, so it was very easy for me to ignore it.

We arrived in Germany and I almost didn't sleep. The fly attendant came to me and asked what food I would want:

— Chicken or Pasta? – She asked (in English).

I actually didn't know the word "pasta" at the time. I knew I liked chicken, so I chose chicken. After a few minutes we arrived at the airport and left the plane. I saw Sister Galdino and we started to talk.

— I didn't know what Pasta was – I mentioned.

— Me neither! – Sister Galdino said. She also had very good English – So, I asked Pasta to see what it was.

Interesting, her approach was the opposite of mine. She then told me what pasta was, in Portuguese we just call it "macarrão", but the literal translation would be "massa". All of us walked around the airport and found the place where our last flight would be. We still needed to wait a few hours, so we went to a McDonald's to buy some food. I wasn't hungry, but I knew that if I bought something with one of my dad's credit cards (that he gave me for my mission) he would receive a notification on his cell phone. I bought ice cream just so my family would know I had arrived safely at my first stop.

Later they told me that it was exactly what happened, but they were also following the flights on the internet.

After waiting for a few hours, we boarded our last flight headed to Nagoya. This last flight also took around ten hours and it was even harder for me to sleep. Maybe I was too nervous to sleep. When we were closer to Japan, the flight attendants gave me a piece of paper with pieces of information for me to answer.

I could read everything, but I wasn't sure what I should write for many of the questions. I would try my best, so I said a small prayer, asking the Lord to help me to write the correct information, and grabbed a pen.

— Hey, Irineu! – Someone whispered next to me.

I turned to my left and Elder Cavalcanti was there crouched next to my chair.

— I talked with Sister Galdino and Elder Orsi and we found the correct information – He told me what I should mark.

— Thanks Cavalcanti – I said.

— No problem, I will talk to Sister Rebouças now – And he immediately walked away.

I smiled and was surprised with how quickly and directly the Lord answered my prayer. In the tiny television in front of me, I could see where the airplane was, and, since we were already in Japan, I could see an animation of the flight above many towns. One of the towns caught my attention because it was called "Inuyama", similar to an anime I used to watch with my siblings called "Inuyasha". I had no idea, at the time, but that city would be important to me.

After that, we arrived in Japan and walked on the airport. We needed to talk with some people and explain our purpose in the country, that kind of thing.

We all said our farewell to Sister Rebouças, and she left to take another flight to Sapporo. On the line, I was closer to Sister Galdino and we started talking with another woman. She was also from Brazil and was traveling to Japan because she had family there. Since she asked who we were, we explained to her about the Church of Jesus Christ of Latter-Day Saints. She had heard about the church before and was surprised that our religion also existed in Japan. Before going away she said she would look for the church close to her family.

She gave a big hug to Sister Galdino and came to hug me too. I kindly explained to her that Elders shouldn't hug women and shook her hand, saying that it was a pleasure to meet her.

Elder Orsi saw the whole thing and came to me:

— I think you could've hugged her. She was already an older woman – He mentioned.

— No. I'm not going to break a rule the same day I arrived on my mission – I answered feeling no guilt.

At the airport, I received a document that it was my official ID for my time in the country. We left with our luggage and it was easy to see some missionaries waiting for the four of us. There were two Elders and a missionary couple.

They greeted us in a very excited way and asked us how our flight was. We talked with them, and I soon learned that the Elders were the Mission President's Assistants: Elder Gish, and Elder Souza. They were both very pleasant and friendly. The missionary couple was Elder and Sister Straton. They asked us if we had our bags with everything we would need for the next couple of days (like the President requested in his letter). After we told them that we had, they sent our luggage right there to our mission areas. President Ishii had already chosen our areas, but they obviously wouldn't tell us yet.

Sister Straton told us that we needed to eat something before anything and we went to a "Subway" to order food. After eating, we would go to the Mission's Office (or "honbu", as the missionaries used to call it). Sister Galdino went in a car with the Stratons, we went to a big car there with the Assistants.

The Japan Nagoya Mission used bikes (and that would be somewhat of a problem to me in the beginning), but the Assistants were the only missionaries who also had cars to help the President. The car had seven seats, so all of us could enter it.

The first thing I noticed was that the car's steering wheel was on the right side, the opposite from my country. That was so interesting! I knew that people drove on the opposite side in England, but had no idea that it was the same in Japan.

The assistants drove us to the Mission Office that stayed in the area of Meitou (in Nagoya). Japan was beautiful, I couldn't see much more than some streets, houses, and buildings, but everything was clean and organized. The sky was blue and with a bright sun. The cars were a little smaller than the ones in Brazil, but many of them also existed in my country.

Elder Gish and Souza explained that President Ishii was doing something important and had to leave town, that's why he wasn't at the airport to receive us, but he would arrive soon at the honbu. There were some missionaries going away and we talked to some of them.

It was weird how early it looked. I had been traveling for over 24 hours. I entered the São Paulo airport in the afternoon (although my flight departed at night), arrived at the Frankfurt airport in the morning, and arrived at Nagoya again in the morning. It felt so weird.

Soon, President and Sister Ishii arrived and shook our hands with a great smile. We would all have interviews with him. President Ishii was Japanese, but he was fluent in English, so we would all talk in English. Elder Cavalcanti unfortunately didn't know English, he arrived at the MTC not knowing any English, so he was studying a lot every day to learn English and Japanese. It was especially hard for him because all of our materials to learn Japanese were written in English.

Gladly, Elder Souza told us that he was Brazilian, but had been living in the United States for years before going on a mission. So, he could translate for Elder Cavalcanti.

My interview with President Ishii was very good, he asked many things about me and my travel. At one point he asked if I was the only member of the church in my family or not.

— My parents and my siblings are also members of the church – I answered.

— Were your parents the first ones to be baptized?

— Yes. They were both baptized when teenagers.

— So, you are the second generation of church members in your family? – He asked with a smile.

— Yes – I answered. I never thought about that. I suppose so. How nice, it was probably more common in Japan to count the generations.

The Mission Office was a white building with three floors right next to a church building, the church of Meitou. Later I saw that next to the Mission Office there was a big house, and that house was connected to the white building. That house was the home to the Mission President and his wife.

They all guided us to the second floor where there was a hallway with many doors, each door was a room with three beds. Me, Elder Orsi, and Elder Cavalcanti would sleep in one of those rooms later that night. Since it was still the afternoon, we would do some missionary work later with two other Elders, but they left us for a while.

We were all so tired that we laid down in the bed for a little while. We were still in our suits and knew that we couldn't sleep yet.

— I'm so tired! I think I might end up sleeping – Elder Orsi said with a little of concern in his voice.

— It's OK. Cavalcanti will never let us sleep – I answered looking at the ceiling. Cavalcanti was in the bathroom at that moment and would come back soon. He loved to follow every mission rule, so there was no need to worry.

We both laughed and immediately after that, I fell asleep.

Someone called for us and I woke up. Through the window, I could see that the light was weaker. Two Elders that I didn't know had entered the room and woke us up. Elder Orsi and Cavalcanti were at the beds next to mine, and they were both sleeping as well.

— We slept! – I said surprised.

— A lot – One of the Elders said with a smile.

— You were very tired from the travel, so Sister Ishii told us to let you sleep – The other Elder explained.

I was very glad that Sister Ishii told them to let us sleep. The two Elders introduced themselves, the shorter one was called Elder Osmund, and the tall one was called Elder Gentry. They told us that we would have dinner in a nice place and we walked with them to the street.

We walked around many streets and passed by many people. The two missionaries said happy "Hello" to every single person walking on the street, and that made people smile. Seeing them greeting unknown people made the three of us to wave to the people as well.

Everything was so different in that country. As I mentioned, the cars were different and usually smaller, but the streets, the stores, everything was different. Everything was also beautiful, but I also couldn't read most of the signs and names on the buildings.

Many times the signs were written in Japanese but had an English translation beneath it. That helped a little bit. We went to a big restaurant called "Sushiro". The two Elders said that we could eat as much as we wanted because they would pay. Elder Cavalcanti and Orsi were very excited and I pretended to be too.

The only problem is that I never liked sushi. I was the only one of my siblings that didn't like sushi. But the Elders were being very kind so I was determined to eat as much as Elder Orsi and Cavalcanti and pretend to like.

Gladly, it wasn't necessary to pretend. When I ate, I loved it. Maybe the sushi from Brazil was much worse or maybe the Lord quickly blessed me to like the food from Japan. I was happy with both options (but after coming home I also liked the sushi from Brazil, so it was probably the second option).

The five of us sat in a rectangular table and many plates were constantly passing on our right side. We could just reach and peak a tiny plate with two pieces of sushi. When we finished the sushi we staked all the tiny plates in a big tower. The worker from the restaurant brought a big wooden ruler and measured the amount of plates, then she told us how much it was.

Each plate was worth around 100 or 200 yen, except for special plates that had a different color and were more expensive.

After we left the restaurant they told us that we would do some proselyting (the word in Japanese for that was "dendou", and sometimes missionaries would speak the Japanese work as an English verb like "We were dendouing" or sometimes: "let's do some dendou"). Elder Gentry left with Elder Orsi and Cavalcanti and Elder Osmund and I went on a different direction.

As soon as Elder Osmund stop someone on the street I knew that I would still need to study and pray a lot to understand Japanese. He had a nice conversation with a man, and I didn't understand the most part. He usually introduced me to the person and I told them who I was:

— Irineu Chourou desu. – I said. In Japanese, Elder was "chourou".

We kept walking and we went to a very dark street with no one around. In Brazil, I wouldn't walk on that street that late at night. But I always heard that Japan was very safe. And even in Brazil missionaries walk in dangerous places that most people avoid.

— So, Japan is very safe, right? – I mentioned, just to be sure.

— Oh, Yes. I never heard of a missionary getting mugged in Nagoya – Elder Osmund quickly said – Is it the same in Brazil?

— Not at all – I answered with a smile. Although Brazil is not as dangerous as many Japanese people think (I would later learn that), mugging is sadly much more common there – But it is very common for people to respect the missionaries and many criminals avoid mugging the missionaries.

— That's nice – He said impressed.

On our way back to the Mission President's house, There was a man walking in our direction. He probably wasn't much older than us.

— We should talk to him – Elder Osmund whispered – Excuse me, can we talk to you for a second?

I did understand Elder Osmund's question in Japanese, but I was shocked that the man immediately stopped and calmly said:

— Sure!

From what I learned with Sister Uchiyama in the MTC, no one would stop to talk to us. But the Japanese people were much nicer and much more polite than everything Sister Uchiyama said. I think she was trying to get us ready for difficult situations and people with closed hearts (that exist anywhere in the world). And I was later grateful to her for that.

The man and Elder Osmund had a nice conversation (that I failed to understand most of it), and in the end Elder Osmund asked him if we could pray with him.

— Can you say the prayer? – He asked me with naturality.

— Me? – I asked surprised. I had never prayed in the street with a stranger – Sure!

I then said a prayer, just like I had learned in the MTC. By the end, the man was very impressed with my Japanese, especially when Elder Osmund told him that I had arrived that day. But Japanese people are extremely kind, especially when they see that you are trying to speak their language. Honestly, I think they are an example of how we should treat anyone who is trying to learn a new language, but I didn't know this back then, so his compliment made me very happy.

We came back to the President and Sister Ishii's house and I saw that more missionaries had arrived. They were the missionaries coming from the Provo MTC. It made sense we would all arrive at different times. There were three missionaries: Elder Mcbride, Sister Akazawa, and Elder Wada.

At the end of the night, we all sat on a big L-shaped couch in the living room and President Ishii explained that on the next day, they would explain everything about the mission to us. We would also meet our first companions, our trainers, and go to our areas.

I took a shower before going to my room. Even the Shower in Japan was very different. When I lay in bed, I looked at the ceiling and started feeling very nervous, almost afflicted. For the first time on my mission, I thought "This is crazy". Probably I was just very tired, but it just hit me that I was in a completely different country. Brazil was very far and 12 hours away from me. I couldn't even talk to people, because I still needed to learn Japanese. At that moment, I felt completely lonely.

"It's Ok. I only need to resist for 22 months", I told myself. Counting on months helped me to feel better somehow.

I tried not to feel more nervous about meeting my new companion on the next day or leaving for my first area. Ignoring all of these thoughts, I closed my eyes and slept.

6

Inuyama

The next day, I woke up less worried than I felt the night before. I guess sleeping always helps a little bit. It wasn't hard to wake up early, for any of us. Maybe we were too excited, but it could be the time difference being a problem for us. After all, Japan is twelve hours ahead of Brazil.

Either way, all the new missionaries sat in the living room and President Ishii, along with other missionaries started to explain the mission to us. It was so much information (all of it important), that I started to worry about remembering everything.

Every missionary house had a "Go-Bag" ready in case a natural disaster happened. It was our job to make sure the "Go-Bag" had all of the necessary materials, including food, water, medicaments, and other things. This part seemed pretty easy to me. A more complicated part was regarding trash. The way of disposing of trash was different in each city of Japan. Also, there were specific days and locations to dispose of dry trash, organic trash, and even more specific information about specific materials. Each of these information changed depending on the city in which you lived. So, we would need to ask our companions about it.

The next part was about bikes. The missionaries in Japan used bikes and I knew that would be a problem later during my time on the

MTC. Now the time had come. I had brought money from Brazil to buy my bike, but the missionaries in the honbu told me that I could take one from the Mission and I was very grateful to them. Still, I did not know how to ride a bike.

I tried to learn before going to the MTC but didn't have a lot of success. I could ride the bike in a straight line. Hopefully, that would help. They explained the dangers of riding a bike and all of the physical and legal accidents that could happen (that was terrifying to me), and later told us to always use a bike shop called "Asahi", simply because it was a great brand and existed everywhere.

Later they showed us the mission zones. The Japan Nagoya Mission was very big and took the central part of Japan. There were many prefectures and cities and we usually traveled by train. This part of the presentation made me very excited to leave and see everything with my own eyes.

I started wondering when our companions would arrive. Would they enter at the end of the presentation and introduce themselves? Would I like my companion? Elder Cavalcanti and Elder Orsi mentioned that they were afraid of having a Japanese companion who wouldn't know English and would make communication hard. We came to the conclusion that this would, at least, be good for us learning the language.

President Ishii also mentioned that we would need to have a "White Mon". He explained that Japan had some large numbers of money. The highest coin was a big, golden (beautiful) coin of 500 yen. On paper there were 2,000 yen bills, 5,000 yen and the highest was 10,000 yen bills.

This last one was called a "White Mon", and it was very important for every missionary to have an extra one. This way, in an emergency, we would have enough money to go back to the Mission Office (honbu).

There was no way of knowing at the moment, but later on in my mission, the White Mon would be indeed very important.

President Ishii also taught us a few things and explained that, as missionaries, we should have joy. We were sharing the gospel with every person that we could and the gospel was about the "Plan of Salvation" or "The Plan of Happiness", as the scriptures also call it. So, we should represent the Lord and have fun in our daily lives, as long as the Spirit can always be our personal companion. We should never do anything that sends the Holy Ghost away from us.

Finally, the presentation was over, and President Ishii said:

— Now, let's go meet the trainers!

I think we all looked a little nervous and excited at the same time. We left the Mission President's home and walked the short distance to the Meitou church building. There, we entered the sacrament room and there were seven missionaries singing a hymn. They all had big smiles and were singing very well.

Then we sat at the first roll on the right side of the room. President Ishii then went to the stand and started to say some words.

— It's much more ceremonial than I imagined – I whispered to Sister Galdino.

— Yes – She agreed with her head.

I honestly had believed that an Elder would just walk to me and say: "Hello! I am your new companion". But no, President Ishii announced on the Stand the area and the new companions. The two missionaries would go up, hug, and then sit together. I was never a big fan of hugs, but missionaries used to hug a lot. Sisters and Elders never hugged, of course, it was a rule. But Elders hugged each other pretty often.

— Elder Cleaver and Elder Irineu will serve in the Inuyama ward – President Ishii announced.

I walked to the stand, close to President Ishii, and hugged my new companion. Elder Cleaver was about the same height as me and was red-haired. He seemed to be very nice and after the meeting, we took a picture pointing to our area on the map. Inuyama was close to

Nagoya, it was in the same prefecture, Aichi. It was interesting how I had seen this city on the airplane, arriving in Japan.

We all had lunch with our trainers at the Church building.

— Do you know how to ride a bike? – Elder Cleaver asked me.

I hesitated.

— Well... I didn't know, but I started to practice after receiving my mission calling. I'm still not very good – I explained.

— But you know something – He guessed.

— Yes.

— It will be fine then – He said it with confidence.

I was worse than I thought, though.

— I brought some money from Brazil, but it's not in yen. Do people use dollars in Japan? – I asked. I actually had brought dollars because my family thought it would be better than reais to use in Japan.

— We will need to trade it for yen. But it's not hard – He said – After we leave, we can stop in a bank before arriving at Inuyama.

I still needed to do many things before leaving the Mission Office. My luggage was on its way to Inuyama, so I only had a backpack. However, I also bought with Elder and Sister Straton new sheets for my "futon", the "beds" people (and all missionaries) use in Japan. After this, Elder Cleaver and I talked with other missionaries at the honbu to receive my helmet and new bike.

It was a blue, thin, light bike. Seemed good to me, but I also didn't know anything about bikes, so I would never complain anyway. I also received a "bike bag" something we would need to use when traveling with our bikes. Elder Cleaver told me that he would show me how to put the bike in it when we got to the train station.

I got all of my things and said goodbye to Elder Orsi.

— You and Elder Orsi were MTC companions? – Elder Cleaver asked.

— Yes.

— My MTC companion also came to Japan Nagoya with me, but I haven't seen him since we arrived on the mission – He commented.

— Really? – I was impressed. That meant I probably wouldn't see Elder Orsi again for a really long time, maybe for the rest of my mission since Elder Cleaver was probably a much older missionary.

We walked down the street heading to the train station. Elder Cleaver and I immediately started talking to each other. He seemed to be someone nice, and I quickly realized that it would be easy to get along with him.

Once we arrived at the train station, Elder Cleaver walked with me to a machine close to a wall. There, he showed me how to buy a "Manaca" card. I could use this card to pay for train passages and even bus passages. I bought the card and put some money into it.

Then, Elder Cleaver showed me how to put the bike inside the "bike bag". I had to unscrew the front tire and tie it to the side of the bike, then I would put the bike on the top of the bag and close the whole thing. After this, I had to carry the bike with my hands. Gladly the bike wasn't very heavy.

We walked a few stairs and got on a train. It was my first time riding a train and I really liked it. In Brazil, I usually used cars or buses. People in Japan were usually shorter than me, and that was easy to notice because there were ads in the middle of the train that would hit me (and Elder Cleaver) in the head, so we needed to duck when walking.

Elder Cleaver knew exactly where we were going, so I just followed him when we left the train, walked to the train stations, and entered on a different train. Eventually, we left the train station and went to a bank. We entered the bank and Elder Cleaver talked to a woman at the front desk.

— Excuse me, we need to trade money. My friend has dollars and he needs to switch to yen – I understood some of what he said. It was easier to guess what he said since I knew what he was going to ask.

— I'm sorry – The woman said with honesty – We only trade money until 5 pm.

I immediately looked up to a big clock behind her and Elder Cleaver did the same. It was 5:02 pm.

— It's 5:02 pm. – Elder Cleaver pointed out. We were only two minutes late.

— Yes, I'm so sorry – She said with an honest expression.

Elder Cleaver seemed to be as impressed as me, but there was nothing we could do, so we left the bank and took another train to Inuyama. This whole experience showed me something of the Japanese culture, they were very obedient to rules and norms, and very rarely made any exception.

Once we arrived at Inuyama we went to a big staircase that had a small and narrowed road in the middle for people to walk their bikes. It was impressive how bikes were an important part of the Japanese culture. So many people walked on their bikes on the streets and, from what I had seen, every high school student had a bike and used it to go to school.

The fact that I didn't know how to ride a bike was probably very weird for a Japanese. Maybe for an American as well.

After we went down the stairs, I saw Inuyama for the first time. It was a beautiful city. On the floor, right in front of the train station, there was a big and beautiful drawing of the Chinese horoscope calendar, with drawings of many animals in the right order.

The street right in front of me had a roundabout with a small garden in the middle and a pyramid as a big statue.

— Welcome to Inuyama Elder Irineu – Elder Cleaver said with a smile – Our house is very close to the train station, so we can walk there.

We walked on the sidewalk for a while. The street was clean, and beautiful, and had some art every once in a while. The art couldn't be described as statues of anything, but they were some modern pieces of metal and rock.

— Inuyama is a very beautiful city and, as you can see, it has some very eccentric pieces of art in the street – He casually mentioned as we walked. I laughed since it was exactly what I was thinking.

We walked in a straight line for a while and then I saw a big store on my right side. It had a big, tall tower with the name "Daiso" written in Japanese (Katakana).

— This store is very useful. It has a little of everything and most of it costs a dollar – He explained.

While we were walking, Elder Cleaver told me some things about my new area and some mission rules. As missionaries, we should talk with everything on the street and share the gospel with anyone and everyone, but Elders could only approach men and Sisters could only approach women. It was an important rule. Talking with any person on the street or wherever we were was called "OYM" in our mission, it meant: Open Your Mouth.

Elder Cleaver explained that we had a lesson soon. There was a member of the church who asked to have lessons with us since he was recently returning to the church. Immediately after the lesson, we had to teach "Eikawa". I had heard about Eikawa on the MTC, it was an English class that missionaries taught for free in the church building for members and non-members of the church. It was a great missionary tool since in the end of every class, the missionaries (us) shared a short message about Jesus Christ.

Our house was very close to the "Daiso" store and was two streets in front of the church building. It was very well located, really. I went to our tiny parking lot for bikes (from our building) and locked my new bike there. While I was locking it, two women passed in the street in front of was really fast and said very friendly:

— Hi, Elders!

— Hello! – Elder Cleaver answered.

I was busy locking the bike, so when I stood up to say hello, they were already gone.

— Who were they? – I asked.

— The Sisters. Don't worry, you will meet them on Eikawa.

— So, there are Sisters in this area too – I was surprised. For some reason, I just imagined that there were only Elders in Inuyama.

— Yes. They actually live in the apartment above us.

— Really? – Another surprise. Although, it made sense to me that the missionaries lived close to the church.

The lesson with the member was great. I was not able to talk much to him, but I shared my testimony with him and after the lesson, I helped Elder Cleaver to set the room ready for our Eikawa lesson. There were many people going to the English lessons in Inuyama, so there were two classes, one for advanced English and one for basic English. That day we were going to teach basic English and the Sisters taught the advanced class.

As we were putting all the chairs in the right place, Elder Cleaver mentioned:

— Are you OK? You're probably very tired – He seemed a little worried.

— I'm great! – I answered honestly.

— Really? You just made a really long trip to get here and had no time to rest.

— True, but I don't really feel tired – I answered very surprised to notice that I was fine.

Many people arrived at the class and Elder Cleaver took the lead role teaching the class. I introduced myself to everybody and sat at the table next to the others. It would be useful to see how Elder Cleaver taught the class. This way I would be able to help more in the next class.

I was paying attention, but for the first time that day, I was just sitting, without needing to concentrate on the information he was saying. I didn't even notice that I started sleeping.

I opened my eyes and saw that Elder Cleaver was the only one who noticed I was snoozing.

— Oh Elder, you are tired – Elder Cleaver smiled. By the look in his eyes, he thought it was funny that I was snoozing in the class.

After the class was over, I officially met the Sisters. One of them was short and had very short blonde hair. The other was taller and had long black hair. Many members of the church were also there and introduced themselves. I talked to them and told them where I was from. I also did my best to memorize everyone's names. But there were too many people at the same time and I just realized I was very tired. I ended up not memorizing the name of anyone (despite my best efforts).

After everything was over, we walked to a close convenience store (called "combini" in Japan) and bought some food to go with the rice Elder Cleaver said we had at home.

— I'm so sorry we don't have better food, but I didn't have time to cook and we didn't have time to go to a restaurant – Elder Cleaver apologized. He seemed disappointed that our dinner wasn't going to be anything special.

— It's OK. Don't worry. I'm not even hungry – I answered with honesty.

Maybe he didn't believe me since I also had said that I wasn't tired an hour before. But it was true, I wasn't hungry at all.

We entered our apartment on the ground floor. Between the front door and the apartment floor, there was a square made for us to take off our shoes, it was called "genkan", and it was part of the Japanese culture not to use shoes inside our houses.

— This is our apartment. We are very blessed to have such a nice place – Elder Cleaver said and showed me the whole place.

On the right side of the genkan, there was a bathroom, with only the toilet there (In Japan there are always two places for the bathroom, one with the toilet and a different one with the shower and sink). In front of the bathroom were the living room and kitchen (it was impossible to say where the room ended and where the kitchen started). On the right side of the living room, there was a place with two tables for us to study and my wardrobe. On the right side of that office, was our bedroom. The floor was of a different material called "tatame" and our futons were there. After the kitchen was the bathroom (the place with the shower, the washing machine, and the dryer for our clothes). Finally, there was also a small room with many materials for our proselyting, including Books of Mormon in many languages, pamphlets, and many other things.

The apartment was actually pretty small, but it looked perfect to me. I had no idea what to expect and that looked great.

That night, I went to sleep and couldn't believe I was in Japan. I also couldn't wait to learn everything I could. There was so much to do the next few days, it was almost overwhelming.

7

A New Mission President and a New Bike

The next day was my first time waking up in Inuyama. The routine of a missionary on the mission field was very different from that of the MTC. We had to work out and do other things to get ready for our day, including planning our day, studying the scriptures, our companionship study, and our language study.

Something that got me by surprise was that, as I was unpacking, I found a small pocket in my backpack that I had never used (or so I thought). Inside that discreet pocket was my MTC padlock. I had no recollection of putting it there, so it was no surprise I had not found it before.

On that first morning waking up in Inuyama, I walked to the food we had and noticed that we had dozens of cereal boxes, all of them closed.

— Wow, you really like cereal — I was impressed.

— Actually, I don't like cereal, that's why we have so many. My last companion also wasn't a big fan and the members give us cereal every once in a while — Elder Cleaver explained.

— You don't like cereal?

— Not really. I think I am the only American who doesn't like cereal.

I was thinking the same thing. All the missionaries who came from the United States loved cereal in the MTC. But no problem, it meant more cereal to me, and I was OK with that. Later on the same morning, I saw a piece of paper on the wall that had information about the trash. That reminded me of what sister Straton mentioned about the different ways of disposing of trash in different cities.

— Elder, what are the days to dispose of trash? – I asked.

Elder Cleaver smirked.

— Nice! You've been paying attention to Sister Straton – He said in a funny tone.

He explained to me how the trash worked, we needed to clean the dirty things that would go to be recycled and there was a day in the week for that. Organic trash was more often, but there were other types of trash, such as milk boxes, that we needed to clean, open, and put on special trash that was only available in a place next to our house a few specific days in the month.

That afternoon, we decided to check my abilities on the bike. Surprisingly I couldn't even stand on the bike. After I tried to ride it, I immediately fell to the ground.

— That's weird, I don't think I am that bad! – I told him.

— Let me check that bike – Elder Cleaver rode the bike for a few seconds – I think I understand the problem. Try to ride my bike.

Elder Cleave's bike was very different from my bike. His bike was bigger and the tires were also larger. On his bike, I was able to ride better and for a longer time (in a straight line).

— The bike you received from the honbu is for more experienced people. It is harder to balance yourself on it – Elder Cleaver explained.

That was a problem. I was already bad at riding the bike and the one I had was especially harder for me. Apparently, it was the type of bike the people used to go really fast. That was not my goal.

— I can buy my bike and choose one more similar to yours – I said.

— I think that would be a good idea.

— Don't you think it will be ungrateful of me to say I don't want this bike anymore? – I asked a little concerned – I mean, what are we going to do with this bike?

— Don't worry, it will be fine. We just need to explain and return it – He responded patiently.

In order to buy my bike, I would need to trade my money for yen, but we decided to take care of that on P-day. Elder Cleaver called the Mission Office and asked how we could return the bike (but gladly, I could keep the helmet). The assistants were coming to Inuyama on Sunday, so they would take care of the bike. I was very glad no one was upset.

As a matter of fact, Cleaver was very patient in general and, like Elder Orsi, he had a great sense of humor. He was very funny and very sarcastic, it was easy for us to get along. He even taught me a word in English: "sassy". And always said I was very sassy. Every once in a while, after I said something, he would answer: "Hey Elder, I don't need your sass!" and I laughed a lot at that.

Later I would learn that having a happy companion was a blessing. But even during those first days, I was grateful for having a good trainer, because I started to feel very lonely. That feeling that I had on my first night in Japan didn't go away and I started to pray very hard for the Lord's help. Feeling lonely was something new for me since I always had been so close to my family, but maybe being so far from them for the first time in my life was one of the reasons I was feeling this way.

As I prayed with faith, I started to feel, or even better, to recognize the Lord's help. It is hard to describe, but I felt very strongly that He was close to me, every day. He personally knew me and always heard all of my prayers. That gave me a much stronger testimony that God is our Heavenly Father, that He loves us, and that He listens to our prayers. And that is how I overcame this feeling of loneliness, by realizing that the Lord was always with me.

Since I didn't have a bike anymore, we walked anywhere we needed to go for the first few days. We talked a lot while walking and if we needed to go to a different city (and we often needed it because our area was very big), we took a train. Walking in the city I noticed that there were a lot of crows in Japan.

— There are so many crows! - I mentioned to Cleaver - It's even a little creepy.

— Why?

— Well, there's always a lot of crows in horror movies or that kind of stuff – I explained.

— Are there no crows in Brazil? – He became curious.

— I never stopped to think about it... I guess not. At least, not in the places where I lived – I would have to ask my family about that.

Later that night, we were walking at night on the street. There was no one on the street and we were walking to teach a new person that we had found. As I was lost in thoughts, I started whistling, a habit of mine.

— Elder, there's something I need to tell you about Japan – Elder Cleaver said carefully.

— What? – I was very curious.

— People don't whistle outside. It's not polite. Especially at night – He said calmly.

— Really? – I was very surprised.

— Yes. It's actually very bad. Everyone will be uncomfortable – He said with a smile.

— That's good to know. I'll have to control myself – I said thinking it would take a lot of attention not to whistle – Why is it a bad thing?

— I heard there's a legend that attracts bad things – He said vaguely.

A few days later, I asked a man in Eikaiwa, why it was wrong to whistle at night.

— It's because of an old legend – He said – Many years ago, people believed that it would attract demons.

— How interesting – I said.

Elder Cleaver and I were outside the church with him and it was around 20:00.

— Do you believe in that? – Elder Cleaver asked with a smile.

— Of course not – He quickly answered.

Elder Cleaver immediately started to whistle.

— No, please stop! – The man quickly asked.

We all laughed, including the man. After that, I never whistled outside anymore, not even during the day. Respecting the culture is very important if we are living in another country. Some months later I asked a Japanese Elder and he said that he had heard that whistling at night attracted snakes, not demons. Either way, it wasn't good.

Inuyama was not an urban area, it was pretty rural. But the church there was a ward, not a branch. I quickly started to try to do some OYMs, which meant to stop people on the street and talk to them about the gospel. It was much harder than I imagined it would be.

Back on the MTC, there had been two Saturdays when we left and tried to make contacts on a big street in São Paulo. It had been hard for me back then, so I knew I would have to overcome it. Elder Cleaver was very patient and helped me to make goals for a minimum of people I would stop by myself.

He was very inspirational about me being bold and standing up for myself. I constantly prayed asking for the Lord's help. I always had been very shy, but in Inuyama I made a goal to become outgoing and brave when preaching the gospel. Slowly I started to make progress.

One day, Elder Cleaver and I were knocking on doors on a street and I rang a bell. A man was walking close to us, so Elder Cleaver walked in his direction and started a conversation. I waited at the door and talked with the person who answered.

The person said she was not interested in learning about any religion, so I used my finest Japanese to ask if she was interested in the free classes we were teaching in English. She was, in fact, more interested and I gave her a pamphlet of Eikaiwa. She closed the door and I turned to walk to Elder Cleaver and help him.

However, another person was coming on the same street. I stopped that person and talked to him. After I finished talking to him. Elder Cleaver came very surprised.

— Irineu, you did great!

— What?

— You totally managed to hold conversations in Japanese all by yourself, two different times with two different people! – He seemed very proud.

— Thank you – I said with a smile.

I was pretty happy with that, once he pointed it out. I guess I was making progress in the language as well. My initiative to stop someone by myself instead of trying to enter his conversation also was not something I noticed, but he did.

Elder Cleaver also helped me with my tablet. All missionaries had a tablet, people who gained the tablet from the mission, like the Brazilians, had an iPad, but later we needed to change to a Samsung tablet. Either way, we could use Facebook and another app called "Line" to connect and talk to the people we were teaching. We almost didn't use Facebook and Elder Cleaver and I had a rule among ourselves of never to open Facebook unless we were going to talk to someone we were teaching. Line was very useful for talking with the people of Japan, everyone uses it there.

We also used Facebook Messenger to talk to our families on P-day. But only used emails to talk with friends.

P-day was far better on the mission field than in the MTC. The MTC was always stressful to talk with our families because they counted every second we spent on the computer and if the computer stopped working for some reason (which happened sometimes), it made no difference for the instructor holding the clock. Also, we needed to wake up an hour earlier to eat and go to the temple, but on the mission, we woke up at the same time as always (6:30 am.), and was much easier to talk to my family using the tablet.

My parents received many pictures of my arrival on the mission. Elder and Sister Straton were in charge of creating and posting a "Japan Nagoya Journal" and sent to the parents. They also sent many pictures of me to my parents on the first two days I spent at the Mission Office. Because of all of that, my parents loved Elder and Sister Straton.

On P-day I bought many necessary things for daily life as a missionary and traded my money for yen. We actually only need it to go to the mail to trade the money. It was much easier than both of us thought it would be.

Once I had my money, the next day we took a train to a close by city where there was an Asahi and I could buy a good bike. Elder Cleaver and I took a close look at many bikes and I really wanted his opinion, since he knew more about bikes than me.

— What kind of bike do you want? – Elder Cleaver asked.

— An easy bike to ride that is resistant. This way she will last my entire mission – I answered.

I ended up buying a bike very similar to his but in a different color. My bike was a black mountain bike with blue details. Sadly, the size of the bike to me was an "M" because of my height and they didn't have one my size. The store ordered the bike and I would have to go back the following week to pick it up.

On my second week in Japan, President Ishii's mission came to an end. Mission Presidents serve for three years, and I arrived on the final week of President Ishii. So, in my second week, there was going to be a big conference with more than one zone to meet President and Sister Judd.

Because of that, one night, a trio of Elders came to Inuyama to sleep in our apartment and go with us to another area called Fukutoku in the next morning. It was an interesting experience to have an apartment full of missionaries, especially since the apartment was not very big. They arrived during our Eikaiwa class and joined. The three Elders were called: Elder Sato, Bennet, and Tanner.

I really liked Eikaiwa because most people there could speak English, so I could have nice conversations with members and people who were meeting at the church. During Eikaiwa, one Japanese woman, who was a member, mentioned that her husband was American. Elder Bennet was excited and said:

— That's so cool! My mother's husband is American – He said.

Most of us didn't say anything. So, his stepfather was American.

— Your father? – The woman asked.

— Yes! – He said with a big smile.

Most of the Japanese were too polite to laugh, but all of the missionaries laughed a lot.

— Why don't you just say, "My father"? – One of his companions asked.

He didn't have an answer. Elder Bennet was very funny and I discovered that night that he had a strange taste for food. He told me that one day he didn't have milk in the apartment, so he ate cereal with apple juice. I only didn't talk much to Elder Sato. He was Japanese and didn't know English very well. I, on the other hand, didn't know much Japanese. So, we didn't talk much that night.

The following day, we took an early train and went to Fukutoku. Going there required switching trains a few times and when we finally arrived on the subway, we were so deep underground that we had to go up many sets of stairs to go up to the street. Fukutoku was beautiful. It was a part of Nagoya, so it was very urban, unlike Inuyama, but I really liked the city for some reason.

We walked from the subway to the church, it wasn't a long walk and I was so fascinated with the city that it was easy to memorize the way there. The "Meet the Judds" conference was very good. We all took an individual picture with President and Sister Judd and later we had a devotional, where they introduced themselves.

President Judd was very tall and some people thought he was intimidating before meeting him (similar to President Martins Silva in a way), but he was a very warm person with a big heart. He was strict with the rules, but he genuinely cared about each of us and we could feel it. He also clearly studied a lot the scriptures. He always would ask great questions that really made us think about the gospel and seek more knowledge.

Sister Judd also had a great heart. She was incredibly kind and really cared about us. She always made sure that we would feel loved and I never saw her being rude to anyone. Later I would also learn that Sister Judd was a great cook. She would always bring us a cookie or some other delicious dish during interviews with the President.

Anyway, on that devotional, I saw Elder Cavalcanti, but Elder Orsi and Sister Galdino were not there. I also met many missionaries that I had never seen before. Most of them were really nice. Later I talked to one of them, he turned to Elder Cleaver very surprised, and said (very shocked):

— He has perfect English!

— Thank you – I said with a big smile.

It was a good thing that my English was good because my Japanese needed some work. After we went back to Inuyama, Elder Cleaver showed me how to ask for reimbursement for our train travels.

The following day we were going to make a division (or "koukan", as the missionaries called it in Japanese), we were going to Fukutoku and work with the zone leaders. Usually, the koukan is made with the district leader, but Elder Cleaver was the district leader, so we needed to do the koukan with the Zone Leaders.

Sadly, I didn't have my bike yet, and the Zone Leaders had an appointment with another missionary, so Elder Cleaver and I were going to work together with Elder Horton. He was a very tall, blonde missionary. Because of that, he and Elder Cleaver were very easy to see in Japan. Japanese people always have black hair, if they are fully Japanese and most people are not very tall. So, a redheaded person and a very tall blonde person were easily seen on the street.

Since we didn't have bikes, we had to walk to find a specific person that Elder Cleaver really wanted to find. Apparently, a few weeks ago, the missionaries had found someone who lived in Fukutoku, so Elder Cleaver and Horton were trying to find his address now.

— So, Elder Irineu, what is one thing that you are trying to Improve as a missionary? – Elder Horton asked. It was a normal question, as missionaries we always had a goal for the day, the week, and even the transfer.

— I'm trying to be better at OYMs – I answered honestly – Stopping people on the street is not very easy for me.

— Ok. That's a great goal. OYM is very important.

— Do you have any hints? – I asked.

— Just think you are the weirdest person on the street – He answered.

I smiled and looked at him confused. Interesting advice, I really wanted to hear his logic.

— Just stop to think about it: you came from a different country to a place you didn't choose, to teach people you don't know about God and His Son, Jesus Christ. You are going to teach them about sacred books that contain the word of God (the scriptures) and invite them to be baptized – He explained – No one else is like you on this street and it is weird when you stop to think about it. After you have this very clear in your mind, there's no reason to be shy.

— That's true – His logic was undeniable and a little funny.

After taking a train, walking a lot, and talking to many people, we arrived in a small neighborhood. All the houses had one or two floors and were very beautiful, very classic Japanese. Elder Cleaver was not sure about the address, so we decided to ask someone.

We knocked on a door. An old lady came to the front door and talked to us. They explained the problem to her, showed the address, and asked if she knew where that place was. The small Japanese lady was clearly a nice person. She looked at the paper and started talking with Elder Cleaver and Horton.

She talked a lot. I couldn't understand what she was saying and after a while, it seemed she was saying the same thing over and over again. Since I was not being able to follow the conversation, I stopped paying attention. She just didn't stop talking. After some minutes, Elder Horton said that his phone was ringing and walked a few steps away, asking me to follow him.

— Hello! This is a fake call! – He said in English, very naturally and out loud.

I laughed a little bit while he pretended to talk to someone, it was a good thing the woman didn't know English. Quickly, Elder Cleaver's phone rang.

— Excuse me – Elder Cleaver said to the lady in Japanese and answered – Hello!

— She's a little crazy – Elder Horton said on the phone.

— I know.

— We don't have time anymore to go in the direction she said the person lives – Elder Horton said.

— Yes, we need to head back home.

They hung up their calls and Elder Cleaver thanked the woman for the help but explained that we needed to leave. Apparently, I wasn't so wrong, the woman said that she didn't know where the man lived and pointed somewhere, then kept saying the same thing for about 20 minutes. I was right, she was repeating herself all the time. I needed to be more confident in my Japanese.

We were going to sleep at Fukutoku, but walking it would take us longer to arrive home. Also, I couldn't run. My doctor explained to me that if I didn't want to have problems with my knee, I shouldn't run for a few months and should never play soccer. Playing soccer was not a problem, I never liked soccer, but the other part was a little annoying. I also always wore my knee brace when I knew I was going to walk a lot.

We took a train to head back to the apartment. On the train, Elder Horton was on my right side, and sitting on my left was a Japanese man.

— You know, trains are a great place to start conversations with people. Usually, everybody is bored and has nothing to do – Elder Horton told me – You could try talking to that guy.

— Ok – I said very willing to try it – Isn't rude to talk to other people on the train?

— Not at all. But it is very rude to eat, drink, or talk on your phone – He answered – Very disrespectful.

— Good to know.

I suddenly felt very nervous. Since it would be a quiet conversation, I would have to do everything alone, without help. I prayed very quickly, asking the Lord to help me, and then turned to the man on my side. I said hello and asked him where he was going and he explained he was coming back from work. He naturally asked me where I was going. Elder Horton was right, it was easier to have a conversation on the train!

After some time, he naturally asked why I was in Japan since I was so young. That was a great opportunity to talk about the church and my work as a missionary. Eventually, I asked if I could give him a pamphlet about the Restauration and he agreed, he was curious about the church. Sadly, he didn't live in Inuyama, but I gave him some information about the church and how he could find a ward close to him. After that, he left the train.

I was very happy with that conversation, it was much better than I could have hoped for. I said another silent prayer and thanked the Lord. I was completely sure the Lord had helped me.

The next day, Elder Cleaver and I came back to Inuyama. A person that we were teaching called Niwa gave us a ride to the Asahi place where I bought my bike. It had finally arrived!

— What do you think of going back to Inuyama with our bikes? – Elder Cleaver asked.

— Would we have to ride close to cars? – I asked.

— Yes. There is no sidewalk.

— I can try – I answered. Part of me got really afraid. I really wanted to practice a little bit before riding my bike next to cars on the road.

— No, let's go back using the train – Elder Cleaver said after thinking a little bit.

Maybe the Spirit whispered to him that it was a bad idea.

We arrived at the shop and I finished buying the bike. I also bought a lock for the bike and a good light. The man who sold me the bike walked with us outside the store and started explaining many things about it. He was using very complicated terms related to the bike and explaining how everything worked.

He spoke many things and paused for Elder Cleaver to translate for me. Elder Cleaver started explaining to me about the gears, the brakes, and many other things.

— You understand everything he's saying?! – I was impressed – Your Japanese is amazing!

— Thanks, but I don't really understand everything. I see the part of the bike he's pointing at and then explain what I think he's saying – Cleaver explained.

I did my best not to laugh since the man was finishing his explanation. After buying the bike, we walked to the nearest train station and I put my bike in the "bike bag". On the way home I told Elder Cleaver:

— I just thought the perfect name for my bike.

— What is it?

— Night Fury.

— Like the dragon from "How to Train Your Dragon"? – Elder Cleaver got the reference.

— Yes! It's perfect for the bike since it's black and blue – I said.

I had my bike, now I just needed to learn how to ride it.

8

Dangerous City

Being a missionary in Japan had some big differences from being a missionary in Brazil. One of them was that in Brazil the members give lunch to the missionaries every day, but on my mission, there was no lunch or dinner given by the members. Of course, every once in a while, a member invited us to eat or took us to a restaurant, but usually we needed to cook our Lunch and Dinner. Also, the members gave us a box full of food and ingredients once a month, which was a real blessing.

But sadly, I didn't know how to cook. The only thing I could cook was a dessert that my mom taught me called "Pavê de Sonho de Valsa". Elder Cleaver described it as an "ice cream pie". But Elder Cleaver would teach me how to cook everything he knew. I wrote all of his recipes in a little notebook and also asked my mother for some easy dishes.

Cooking rice was easy because every missionary house had a machine to cook rice. That was extremely useful to us and a real blessing.

I was very happy with Inuyama. The city was very rural and very beautiful. In some places, there were fields of rice as far as the eye could see, but there were also many mountains that I thought were so beautiful I could look at them the whole day. If Elder Cleaver and I went to a tall building, I would take a few moments just to look at the view.

The church in Inuyama was also great. The building had three floors and the sacrament meeting room was on the second floor. The members were extremely kind and polite. The ward mission leader was a Brazilian called Fábio. He was fluent at Japanese, English, and Portuguese (Portuguese was his native language), so he would translate most meetings to other Brazilians from the ward and he always helped Elder Cleaver and I a lot. Sometimes, he would give us rides on his car and help us with lessons.

Another member was brother Endou. He was Japanese but could also speak English, so I used to talk a lot with him. He always asked me: "Elder Irineu, what new grammar are you studying in Japanese?". And after I told him the new grammar or word (or both) he said: "Practice with me". That always made me a little nervous because I didn't want to make mistakes when telling him what I had learned.

Because of that, I always chose one grammar to study really well during the week to be able to use it with brother Endou on Sunday and after Eikaiwa, during the week. I think he was trying to help me, and it really worked. It always kept me motivated to study.

Elder Cleaver also helped me studying Japanese. He had a great Japanese, especially considering that he actually wasn't an old missionary, he was on his sixth transfer when we became companions (one transfer is the same as six weeks). But he was really good with languages in general, he could even understand some Portuguese.

On the Sunday after buying my bike, Elder Cleaver and I went to the church's parking lot to practice with my bike. I was able to ride this bike much better than the one I returned to the Mission, but I still was bad. Gladly, Elder Cleaver was a great teacher and we practiced for a few hours. I was much better by the end of the day.

We started to ride the bike for short distances. It was a good thing that Inuyama wasn't an urban area, this way there were fewer obstacles and fewer people on the streets. It really was a blessing. On the following day, we rode our bikes to go to a McDonald's, but on the way there, I lost control of the bike and fell out of it. My bike flew one or two meters and fell close to a rice field. I fell on the floor.

— Are you OK? – Elder Cleaver asked. He came back after he saw I fell.

— I'm good – I said and felt a pain in my leg. I raised my pants a little and saw that my left leg was bleeding a little bit – Oh no.

— Are you afraid of blood? – Cleaver asked a little worried.

— Not at all – I said and felt glad it wasn't anything serious – Let's go eat.

I got my bike and felt really grateful that it wasn't broken or even scratched. The problem was my bag or better yet, my bag was one of the problems. I had bought a bag in Brazil that I thought would be perfect for a bike, but in reality, it was too big. It balanced me to a specific side and always made me fall.

— I think I need a new bag – I mentioned to Elder Cleaver.

— I agree. It's a beautiful bag, but even I would fall with it – He mentioned.

He was being humble, I think. But I definitely needed a new bag, so on that P-day I bought a new bag that was very common for the Japanese to wear it. My previous bag was very beautiful, so I kept using it to go to church, Zone Conferences, or other places that I only needed to walk to. Using that bag, I fell less. It didn't throw me of balance and that was all I could ask for.

A bag was essential to us because we always needed to carry our tablets, at least one Book of Mormon, and pamphlets (we always carried different pamphlets in different languages). On a good day, our bag was almost empty when we came back home because we gave the pamphlets and even the Book of Mormon to people we found.

One day, Elder Cleaver had an idea. It was the week that we were supposed to practice "housing" (knocking on doors to find people) as part of my training. So, he found a nearby neighborhood that seemed to be perfect for us to knock on some doors and hopefully find new people to teach. It wasn't far if we used a bike, but it was too far to go walking. Which meant it would be the longest distance I had ever used to go using the bike.

I wasn't afraid though, I needed to go wherever the Spirit sent us. Because of that, I was completely willing to go anywhere using my bike. Of course, I was always praying a lot for the Lord to protect me and help me to learn fast how to ride a bike.

We left our house and Elder Cleaver went ahead. I followed on my bike. Soon, we left our town and followed a road that eventually became a highway. I started feeling nervous, I couldn't fall since cars were passing very fast on my left side. Cleaver found another road that crossed a plantation, and we were able to avoid the cars for a while. But eventually it was necessary to go back to the highway.

There, something happened and I fell. Gladly, no car hit me, but I kept going. Elder Cleaver was clearly worried after that and asked:

— Maybe this is too dangerous. Do you want to go back?

— Are we far from the city? – I asked.

He checked the map on his tablet.

— No. We are halfway through.

— Then, last go ahead! – I said with more confidence than I was feeling – It's not worth to go back.

— OK – He answered, and we kept going.

This time, I kept myself on the left side of the road. Not sure why, since it would be the wrong side if it were a two-way street. On that side, the cars were passing really fast on my right side and on my left side there was nothing, only a big fall into a great river. "It's a good thing I know how to swim", I thought to myself but was determined not to fall again.

Many meters after, we reached what seemed to be another city. The only problem was that the road became unbelievable steep. That made my work much harder. My legs were almost hurting from the effort. Elder Cleaver had mentioned that I should use lower gears for this kind of situation, but I couldn't remember what was the right button on my right handlebar. I chose one and pressed twice.

It was the wrong choice. The pedal immediately became much harder and riding my bike became something incredibly hard. The day was also very hot, so I quickly became very sweaty. The road would continue to be steep forever, as it seemed. At that moment, I wasn't only exhausted and afflicted, I also became very angry at myself. It was ridiculous that the bike and the road were completely defeating me, but it was the reality.

Elder Cleaver was long gone, since he didn't see me staying behind. Even if I wanted to follow him, I was not capable of using the bike on that steep terrain. I stopped trying and just stood there, almost feeling like crying because of my frustration.

It probably took only three or four minutes for Cleaver to show up next to me.

— Elder, what happened? – He asked more confused than worried. After all, I was fine, I had only stopped going forward.

— I can't ride the bike. It's probably in gear 7 and it became too hard – I explained very tired.

— I see – He answered – I know what we can do!

He lifted the back tire and I manually spun the pedal while he pressed the button to lower the gear. It was very ingenious, if I had more experience using a bike, I probably would have thought of that. Actually, if I had more experience I would have used the right gear in the first place.

After that, I was able to keep going and Elder Cleaver started going behind me, just in case something happened. Now was perfectly possible to keep going on the steep road, but many more cars started passing next to me and I still was feeling very stressed. Then, I decided to pray, only in my mind. Prayer had always helped me to that moment, so I was sure it would help this time.

"Heavenly Father, please protect me and help me to arrive where we need", I said in my mind (I didn't close my eyes, of course).

That moment, I heard a voice next to me. I'm not completely sure it wasn't on my mind, but it was clear as if someone was speaking next to me: "Be not afraid, only believe". Once I heard those words, that I knew were from "Mark 5:36", I immediately thought about the Savior. Right after that I thought about when Peter was waking on water and felt afraid with the tempest around him. In a way, my situation was similar, I needed to stop feeling afraid and nervous, stop paying attention to the cars next to me, and focus on going forward.

Elder Cleaver always told me not to look down while riding the bike and I was doing that at that moment. It was miraculously easy to stop being afraid and going forward after that. In a very real manner, it was like the Lord blessed me with courage and some optimism. Eventually, we arrived at a place that was the entrance to the neighborhood we wanted to enter. We only needed to go left.

There was a sidewalk now, but the way was even steeper. So, it took a while to go all the way up. "It's like we are climbing a mountain", I thought. And maybe we really were.

— I did it! – I said very happy once the terrain became plain again.

— What a champ! – Elder Cleaver joked – Don't worry, going back will be much easier.

Preaching the gospel there was great and I was able to bear my testimony and even deliver a Book of Mormon to someone. Some time later, we also found a man who wanted to hear about the gospel and we taught him.

Elder Cleaver was completely right about the way back. It was much easier. I didn't even need to touch the pedal to go all the way back to Inuyama. I only needed to be careful about not going too fast and losing control of the bike, but it was easy. At night, the only light on the road was the light of our bikes and I realized that the scenery was very beautiful, there was even a train, very distant, passing by. I could see the lights in the windows and people very distant. It was such a peaceful, happy moment. The worry and frustration I felt a few hours before seemed to be so distant that I felt really grateful to Heavenly Father for His help.

Elder Cleaver and I went back to that place many times later and each time was easier for me. In matter of fact, after that first time, my abilities on the bike improved in a miraculous way. Still, I started calling that neighborhood "Dangerous City", since it was so dangerous for me the first time.

One day I was talking to another missionary on the cellphone and said:

— We were at Dangerous City...

— It's not Dangerous! People are going to start thinking I'm a bad trainer – Elder Cleaver said on the other side of the room – It's also not a city. It's barely a Neighborhood. It's like a tiny, safe suburb.

I laughed a lot, but eventually, he also started calling the place Dangerous City.

One day, leaving Dangerous City, I was going pretty fast on the bike and heard Elder Cleaver screaming behind me. It seemed he was calling me. I safely pressed the brakes and waited for him to reach me.

— Were you calling? – I asked.

— Yes. But it's fine now.

— What was it? – I was curious.

— There was a snake on the road next to you – He said calmly.

— And what happened?! – I didn't see the snake.

— Nothing. You just run over it – He said while moving his shoulders.

— Wow. Ok – I said pretty impressed. It wasn't my intention to kill the snake, but I also wasn't sad about it.

After a few days, I had my first Zone Conference, which, by coincidence, was also President and Sister Judd's first Zone Conference on the mission. Elder Cleaver and I woke up earlier than usual and took a train to the place where the entire zone was going to gather.

The conference was inspired and also very inspiring. President Judd explained some mission rules and shared the new "mission slogan" which was: "In the Japan Nagoya Mission we Teach Repentance and Baptize Converts by doing L³OHTS: We Love the Lord. We Love Our Companions. We Love the People of Japan. We are Obedient. We do Hard Things. We Serve Shoulder to Shoulder."

President Judd explained each of those affirmations. Originally, he thought "We Love the Japanese People", but felt that there are many people in Japan, including foreigners, and we needed to love everyone regardless of nationality. That's why it became "We Love the People of Japan".

Another important point was "We Serve Shoulder to Shoulder". This meant that we were all together in the sacred work of the Lord. No one was better than anyone, we all wanted to help each other and see everyone succeed. President Judd was a great leader and by the end of the Zone Conference, we were always excited to go back to our areas and work hard.

Every Thursday (or on the day it would be most time-effective) we did our DKK (doryou keikaku kai), which was what we called the Weekly Planning Session. That was a time for us to sit down and talk about our work in Inuyama, how we could better work with the ward, and all the members, how we could help better the people we were teaching, what lessons we would teach on that week and on the following week, and stablish more individual goals as well as goals for our companionship.

We always tried not to take too long on this planning, but naturally, it took a few hours, since it was a lot to discuss. Gladly, I had a good relationship with Elder Cleaver, so we didn't need to spend too long talking about what we needed to improve when dealing with each other. But, we always asked something that the other thought we could improve. Some weeks I didn't have anything to say.

— Elder please tell me something I can improve! – Elder Cleaver always asked.

— I'm thinking – I answered honestly and mentally reviewed our last week – I can't think of anything.

— I'm not Jesus! There must be something I can improve!

— I'm sure there is, but I can't think of anything – In my opinion, he was doing a great job in our lessons and with the members – But I'm sure you know the things you need to improve.

— Go die Elder – He said frustrated, and we both laughed.

The next day we worked as we always did. At night, we didn't have any appointments, so we were just talking with people on the street. Eventually, we went to a street not very far from the church, but on the other side of the train station. The sidewalks were very large and there was a convenience store on the other side of the street. It was a nice place to hang out, honestly, and there were five people on the street. They were all men and were about my age or maybe a little older.

Elder Cleaver and I stopped and talked with them. They were all Vietnamese and worked at the same place, so they were good friends. They were also really nice people and very friendly. We talked with them for a long time and gave pamphlets to some of them about the Plan of Salvation, which explains the purpose of life, where we came from, and where we are going after death.

However, one of them was very interested in what we were teaching. His name was Goku (his name was not actually Goku, but his name in Vietnamese was very different and the translation to Japanese, writing it in the alphabet katakana, was Goku) and he was religious, he was also a very smart person who was always seeking knowledge.

To him, we gave a Book of Mormon in Vietnamese (there were many Vietnamese in Inuyama, so one of us always carried one in our bag). They all said they would be in that same place on the next day. They agreed to hear a little more about the church.

The next day we planned what we were going to teach to the people we had appointments with. When we thought about Goku and his friends, we felt that maybe we should teach more about the church first, since they seemed to be more interested in the Book of Mormon than the Plan of Salvation. And that is what we did.

That night Goku told us that he was reading the Book of Mormon and felt something special while he was reading it. "It is a sacred book. I can feel it". He said with a big smile. Even teaching on the street, we all could feel the Holy Ghost at that moment.

9

The Real Teacher

It was the end of July and it was very hot in Japan, or at least in the Japan Nagoya Mission. It was interesting because it was winter in Brazil, but Japan is in the North Hemisphere, so it was Summer. I left São Paulo when the weather was getting a little colder and arrived in Japan during the hottest season.

We invited Goku to go to a Church meeting and even offered to show the church building first. A tour. He said that he wanted to go, but was very hesitant. There are some churches where people speak louder or invite people to stand in front of everybody, and Goku was afraid of that since he was a quiet person. We assured him that no one would invite him to stand anywhere or something like that. He eventually accepted our invitation and said he would go on Sunday.

The next day, a missionary couple visited our apartment. One of their responsibilities was to visit missionaries' houses across the Nogoya Mission to see if we were doing a good job taking care of the apartment and ourselves. They were a very nice Japanese couple and eventually, they asked:

— You know, the best way to take care of a futon is to let it get some sun on P-day. Do you do that? - The Elder asked.

— Actually, we don't. There is a big wasp nest on the balcony, so we never even open those windows - Elder Cleaver answered.

— Really? Let me see – The Elder said.

We walked toward the big window (it was almost a sliding glass door) and they looked at the nest. It was as big as a baseball, though the shape was different.

— Oh, that is easy to solve – The Sister mentioned – All you need is to spray some venom for wasps, then take the nest and throw it away.

We were both shocked by the simplistic explanation.

— I could do it right now. Do you have wasp venom?

— No – Neither of us wanted them to try. They were already elderly, and it seemed a little dangerous.

But it was true that we didn't have anything to kill wasps. After the missionary couple left, we called the sisters and asked if they had any spray to kill wasps. They didn't, but they had one to kill cockroaches.

— If it can kill a cockroach, it probably can kill a wasp – I said.

— Exactly what I was thinking – Elder Cleaver agreed.

We got the spray with the Sisters and made our plan. I was going to open the window, Elder Cleaver would spray the nest, and I would quickly close it. We did that, and I closed the window very fast. Less than a second after I closed the window, several wasps came in our direction and repeatedly hit the window. A few seconds later, they started to fall to the ground and move in very strange ways.

A few seconds after that, there were some wasps on the ground, apparently dead, and the others flew away. We used the same method to spray the nest one more time (just for safety), and then we threw the nest away.

That's how we solved that problem.

Around that time, a member of the church started helping us with proselyting. His name was Jared, he had just finished his mission (at the Japan Nagoya Mission) and was now working there, living in the Inuyama area. He had a car and drove us to a specific neighborhood where we were teaching a very kind old lady.

Jared was American but was very fluent in Japanese. Before teaching the woman, we would knock on some doors in her neighborhood and Jared helped. But I wasn't able to help a lot with the lessons with her, because she had a very difficult way of speaking (or at least I thought so at the time), and sometimes I understood what she was saying, but I didn't know how to say what I wanted. This feeling was unbelievably frustrating and it motivated me to keep studying Japanese. It also helped me to pray with a lot of faith to receive the Lord's help and quickly learn the language.

On the following Thursday, on our DKK, we made a new goal. We would arrive at our apartment exactly at 21:00. Lately we had been arriving 3 or 5 minutes late, and we decided that we needed to be more (and better) obedient.

That same night we went walking to a close by street to talk to people and, when it was around 20:40, Elder Cleaver said:

— I think we should go to the train station.

— But it will be nine hours in twenty minutes, and we don't have our bikes – I pointed. With our bikes maybe we could make it on time, but by walking we would be late.

— I know, but I just have this feeling... – He said looking a little afflicted.

— If you feel that we should go, we should go. It could be the Spirit – I said.

With that decided, we walked toward the train station. It was a relatively long walk, but we arrived there almost at nine. We went up the stairs and there was Goku! He was walking in our direction.

— Goku! It's so good to see you – We said excitedly.

— Wow. It's great to see you too. I was actually going to see the church that you mentioned. It's close, right? – He answered.

— It is! We can go with you and show you the place – We offered.

We walked to the church while talking to him and showed the church. We showed him the place where we had the sacrament meeting, and all the classrooms and explained what we did there. If we had a lesson, it was fine to be 30 minutes late, it was one of the rules.

The next Sunday, he went to church and all the members were really nice to him. Goku was Buddhist, and he really had faith in his religion. As a matter of fact, he understood Buddhism as few people I ever met. He really studied about it and followed his faith. However, he had an open heart and was seeking truth.

He felt that the Book of Mormon was true and started to learn more about Jesus Christ. It is very common in Japan for people to not know much about Christ. Usually in Brazil, everybody knows that Jesus Christ is the Son of God and that he was born of Mary. In Brazil, people also know that God is our Heavenly Father and that He loves us (even if they don't believe in it), but in Japan, this belief is not very common. There, people don't know much about Christ, how He was born, or His commandments.

Later, on July 29th of 2018, a woman that the sisters were teaching got baptized. It was a great and spiritual experience. Many missionaries came for the baptism and Goku saw the ordinance and said that he felt the Spirit in the church.

On the 30th was P-day and my family told me about my brother's wedding. He had gotten engaged to a wonderful girl before I left on my mission, so I knew they would get married during my mission. My Sister, by the way, got engaged while I was at the MTC and married while I was at Inuyama (she married on September 22nd, to be more precise). A part of me felt a little angry that both of them got married while I was on my mission, but I was also very happy for them.

On the first day of August, it was my 100th day as a missionary (I knew it because I wrote every day and kept counting). Elder Cleaver and I celebrated by buying ice cream since Japan had many good and unique types of ice cream.

We kept teaching Goku for the rest of our transfers at Inuyama. It was amazing to teach him because he would tell us about things that he studied in the Book of Mormon and answered his prayers. It became very clear to me that the Spirit and the Lord were the ones who actually converted people. Elder Cleaver and I studied and prepared a lot to teach him about the church, but the real teacher was the Spirit. And such great progress would not happen if Goku didn't have faith and a sincere heart, but he did.

Goku's ability to speak Japanese was as good as mine (approximately) and he didn't know English, so it was very easy to become friends with him since we were both learning Japanese and had similar experiences with the language. Sometimes we needed to use Google translator to understand each other during lessons, but it worked. I will talk more about him soon.

One day we had interviews with the President. We had one every transfer, but we also sent him individual letters every week, so he always knew how we were. In the first interview I had with him we introduced ourselves.

— Elder Irineu, before anything, what is the correct way for me to pronounce your name? – He asked.

I thought it was very thoughtful of him to ask. "Irineu" was a hard word to pronounce for English speakers. Writing in Japanese made the sound of each letter very clear, so it helped missionaries and members. I explained to him and after that, he usually always pronounced my name correctly, but it never bothered me when anyone mispronounced it. It was never a problem for me.

— Let me ask you something, Elder Irineu, do you love the Lord? – He asked me, looking me straight in the eyes.

— I do.

— When was the last time you told Him that?

Strangely, that same morning I was feeling very happy and blessed to be a missionary. That morning, I said a personal prayer thanking for my blessings and told the Lord I loved Him, His gospel, and the scriptures.

— This morning, actually.

— That's the best possible answer – He said with a smile – As I understand you arrived a week before Sister Judd and me, right?

— Yes – I said with a smile.

— That's great. We arrived at the same time, we will serve our missions together – He said with the same big smile.

I felt very happy with that comment. President Judd really taught by example, especially when he said we all serve "shoulder to shoulder". While Elder Cleaver was talking to President Judd, I was talking to Sister Judd. She was very kind and asked me many things about family and I. It was a great conversation. Sister Judd also gave me a cookie that she made and it was made of pumpkin with chocolate drops, it was very good.

It was already my second transfer as a missionary. I was loving Japan and being a missionary. Maybe the only thing that bothered me was that Japan had a lot of spiders. It was amazing, everywhere there was a huge net with a big spider in the middle. Cleaver told me that they disappeared completely during winter and mysteriously came back once the temperature got warmer again.

I guess most people don't care about spiders, but it is one of my fears, and it was something I had to overcome. Amazingly, it happened, after a transfer I didn't care that much about spiders anymore (at least not the small ones, but kept a huge safe distance from the big ones).

One morning, I woke up feeling something strange in my right eye. It was a weird feeling that I didn't really know how to describe. I turned to Elder Cleaver who was folding his futon on my left side.

— Cleaver, is there something wrong with my eye?

He looked at me for a few seconds with a completely inexpressive face.

— No. But I think you should look in the mirror.

If I needed to look in a mirror, there had to be something wrong. I walked to the bathroom and saw that my eye was swallowed with a different color around it. I thought about what could have caused it, but it didn't look like a bite of anything and it also didn't look hurt.

— Cleaver, my eye is not normal! – I said out loud – You told me that it was!

— I didn't want to scare you! – He defended himself.

— What am I going to do?! I never had anything in my eyes! – I asked.

— You should call Sister Judd – He said calmly.

— Ok.

I waited a little bit, because it was very early, and called her after eating breakfast. I explained to her the situation.

— How would you describe your eye? – She asked.

Maybe Cleaver would be better with descriptions since English was my second language, but it was his native language.

— Cleaver, how should I describe my eye?

— It looks like jelly, grape flavor – He answered.

I laughed and heard Sister Judd laughing a lot too.

— You should go to a doctor, especially since it has a different color – She instructed.

— Ok.

— Do you know where you can find an eye doctor?

— Actually, there is one right next to our house, at the end of our street – Cleaver remembered.

He was right, I had seen the place. What an unexpected blessing! There was a very specific doctor just a few meters away from us. We could go walking and it would take less than three minutes.

— Do you think you can understand the doctor? – I asked. I definitely didn't know enough Japanese to talk medical terms, but maybe Cleaver did.

— No. At least, I rather not risk it. I'll call a member – Cleaver answered and took the phone.

We walked to the front of the place and waited for the member. Once he arrived, we walked inside. There, I sat in front of various machines that took pictures of my eye and probably did other things that I couldn't understand and eventually a doctor talked to me. I didn't understand a word that he said, but the member of the church told us that it wasn't anything serious. Something got inside of my eye, and it got infected.

He put something in my eye and gave me two different eye drops, then he told me to use them every day In the morning and at night for two weeks. I called Sister Judd once we got home and explained everything to her. I think she was surprised about me being so positive about the problem, but I was just very relieved that it wasn't anything serious. The brother who translated everything was so relieved with the doctor's explanation that it really made me feel better.

And the doctor was right. That night my eye was already better and after two days it was completely normal.

10

The First Typhoon

On the second transfer, one of the Zone Leaders had changed, so the companionship was now Elder Horton and Elder Kitayama. They were coming to Inuyama for a koukan, where I would spend the day doing missionary work with Elder Kitayama, so I thought it would be a good opportunity to cook my dessert, the "pavê de sonho de valsa". Sonho de Valsa is actually a candy that exists in Brazil, so I would have to change that to a similar candy. Gladly, in Japan, there is a similar candy called "black thunder" which is delicious.

On P-day, Elder Cleaver and I did our best to find all of the ingredients, and that week I cooked it. It didn't get perfect, I would later perfect it cooking it in Japan, but it was pretty close to what it should be. We separated a slice and gave it to the Sisters when we found them. The Sisters were called Sister Macdonnell (we called her "Sister Mac") and Sister Steadham.

Everybody loved the dessert and Sister Mac told me that it was one of the best desserts she ever ate. I think she was exaggerating a little bit, but it was my favorite dessert, the only food I learned before going on my mission. The only one who didn't like was Elder Cleaver, but he didn't say that at first.

— Did you like the dessert? – I asked.

— Of course – It was clearly a lie.

— You can be honest, I won't be mad.

Later that day he caved:

— Ok, I didn't like it. But I'm a little picky with food – He explained.

— It's ok, don't worry – I answered with honesty. Most people liked it, so I was happy.

That day I had the chance to work with Elder Kitayama and learned a lot. He was very good talking to people and it was a fun person to be around. Later that day we were talking about our day (daily analysis) and he said:

— Elder Irineu, you're just so kind!

— Really? – It was an unexpected compliment.

— Of course!

— Thank you!

A little after that, Elder Horton came to me and said:

— Irineu, can I have more of that ice cream thing that you made?

— Sure, it's in the freezer, I'll go get it for you – I answered.

— Thank you. You're so nice Elder Irineu, I bet you'll become a great mission leader – He mentioned.

I thanked him and thought that it was the same compliment that Elder Kitayama made. It was interesting because I never thought of myself as someone kind, it definitely wouldn't be a word I would use to describe myself. But both Elder Horton and Kitayama were very thoughtful, they later bought gifts for Elder Cleaver and me and gave us at the end of the transfer.

A few days later, we decided to visit a city very far of Inuyama, it was still inside our area, but it was so far that we were pretty sure missionaries didn't go there. The name of the city was Shirakawa and the more we thought about it, the best we felt about going there. People In that place probably had never heard about the gospel or met the missionaries.

In most cities, people had seen us before and many people already had opinions about the church. Many times, that's not something bad, actually many times people need to meet the missionaries more than once to give them a chance and hear the message. But as missionaries, it was our job to proclaim to gospel to everyone, and who knows, maybe there was someone there that was seeking the truth but didn't know where to find it.

So, we went to the train station and took more than one train to get there. The city was beautiful. It was small, but it was between the mountains, really close to two of them. That was a big river that crossed the middle of the city and many ducks flew around the place and landed on the waters of the river (It made sense for the town to have a big river around since the name in Japanese means something like "town of the white river"). To enter the city, we had to walk across a silver metal bridge that was really big and interesting.

It was an interesting new experience to teach there. People there had never seen the missionaries and most of them never had heard about the church. Because of that, we taught many people about the gospel, what we believed in and about God.

Unfortunately, since the city was so far away, we needed to start heading back earlier. On our way to Inuyama, in one of the train stations, we started talking to a man. He was really nice and the conversation was so good that we went with him on one of the trains. By the end of the conversation, we even gave him a Book of Mormon.

— Are we going to leave the train now? – I asked standing up.

— Why? – Elder Cleaver looked confused.

— Aren't we in the wrong train?

— No. This is the way to Inuyama – He answered pretty confidently.

— I thought we were on the wrong train and that we just entered to talk with that guy – I explained.

— No, this is the right train.

— Are you sure? – I asked.

— Yes.

— Ok – I sat down and looked at the window. I trusted Elder Cleaver, that was his fourth transfer in Inuyama, so he knew the place really well.

I really liked taking trains, it was really peaceful. As we traveled, I recognized one of the cities, it was a place where we often did some proselyting called Kani.

— I like Kani, it's pretty beautiful – I mentioned.

— We are at Kani?! – Elder Cleaver jumped – We are on the wrong train!

We ran to leave the train at that same stop and took another train to go back to Inuyama, we were indeed going in the wrong direction. I felt happy that I was learning to guide myself better with trains.

On the following day, it was P-day and we had our district activity. I taught people how to make Pastel, a Brazilian food, which was funny because who taught me how to cook pastel was Elder Cleaver, even though it is a Brazilian food (he loved pastel and we were able to buy the right ingredients on a store near to Inuyama). After eating, we visited Inuyama Castle. The cool thing about that castle is that it is an original castle. On World War 2, most castles in Japan were destroyed, but Inuyama has a Castle that survived many wars and has a great history.

On the next day a big typhoon was going to hit Japan. Most people were very nervous about it and the Mission Office told us to stay home and be careful. However, the typhoon would pass far from Inuyama, so Elder Cleaver and I decided to know on some doors close to our house before the weather became dangerous.

I looked at the sky and was very impressed with the clouds. The sky was dark and windy. The clouds were moving so fast that I actually felt a little afraid, I never had seen the sky like that, never had seen clouds behaving that way.

Still, it was safe to walk around. So, we knocked on some doors and introduced ourselves, but almost everybody had the same answer:

— There is a typhoon coming, you should not be outside – They all said with worried expressions.

We realized that wasn't very effective, so decided to head back home. We used our bikes to go back and stopped close to the church. There were wi-fi at the church, so we could do some things that we needed. However, it suddenly started raining and the wind became so strong that we could hear it.

— I think we should go home – I said.

— I agree – He answered and we ran back to our apartment.

It was honestly really boring once we were inside. The rain was strong and so was the wind, all of our windows shook violently every once in a while and I could see the wind moving the rain on the empty streets of the city. But nothing else happened and I spent most of the day reading the scriptures.

I always enjoyed reading the scriptures, so it was kind of nice to have the time to do so, but I rather be outside. I learned that as a missionary I hated to be inside the house. I had to be outside doing something productive, otherwise I just felt bad and often bored.

At night the rain was weaker, but we still had instructions from our leaders to be inside the house. At some moment, the sisters called. Elder Cleaver answered the phone and talked with them for a few seconds, but he mostly heard what they were saying. Suddenly, I heard a lot of screams on the phone.

— What's happening? – I asked very curiously, Elder Cleaver didn't seem to be worried at all.

— We're going – He said and hung up. Then he turned to me – There is a cockroach in their apartment and we have the spray to kill it.

I laughed a lot. We had forgotten to return the spray after the "wasp incident." We walked to their apartment and knocked on the door. They answered and we gave the spray to them. There was, of course, a very important rule that we couldn't enter their apartment, so they needed to handle the cockroach by themselves.

However, at that moment, the cockroach ran toward the door. They screamed and jumped back inside their apartment while the cockroach came in Elder Cleaver's direction. He simply stepped on it and the problem was solved. It turns out that the spray was not necessary, but now they had it and would be able to defend themselves.

Sometime later, I invited one of the people we were teaching to be baptized. The invitation was in Japanese, so I felt very happy once I had been able to do it. We also invited Goku to be baptized and this is how it went:

— So, if I understood it correctly, once I repent and be baptized, I will be cleansed of my sins, right? – He asked.

— Yes – We both answered.

— And baptism is necessary to enter the Kingdom of God, right?

— Yes – We answered again.

— Ok. When can I be baptized? – He simply asked.

We were both very happy with his desire to be baptized. It is very common for people not to understand how important baptism is or how important it is to be baptized with someone that holds the right and authority to do so. But Goku was quickly gaining a great understanding of the gospel and was very smart, so he wanted to be baptized.

However, he wasn't ready to be baptized yet. We still needed to finish teaching many gospel principles and commandments. Also, he still needed to accept some important points of doctrine, since some things were the opposite to what the Lord teaches. For example, if someone believes in reincarnation, the person cannot believe in the resurrection or the atonement of Jesus Christ. We lived as spirits before this life, after we die we go to the spiritual realm and one day we will resurrect in our (perfect) same bodies just as Jesus Christ did and made possible for us to do the same through His atoning sacrifice. This goes against the belief of reincarnation, in which we have many different bodies and pay for our own sins over the span of many different lives.

So, we set a date for him to be baptized and made a goal to be ready by then. We were all very happy that day.

As the days went by, we started talking about the ending of the transfer. That was my last transfer being trained, so Elder Cleaver or I would be transferred for sure, but our only certainty was that we would no longer be companions. Obviously was more likely that Cleaver would be transferred since it was his fourth transfer there.

Part of me hoped that I would be transferred, since it would be my responsibility to explain the entire area, and everything in the Inuyama ward, to my new companion. To me, I felt that was a big responsibility.

On our last week, we had our last district meeting. Elder Cleaver and I walked to the Fukutoku ward. I had already memorized the way there, but it was a very pleasant walk, I loved to take the train and walk on the nice streets to that big church building. We usually used the stairs behind the ward to enter directly on the second floor, where there was a big place with a nice piano, some tables, and a whiteboard.

Elder Cleaver shared a message, we all practiced some techniques related to missionary work and, in the end, we all shared our testimonies. There was a great Spirit there and we all would miss each other, the whole district got along very well. After the last testimony, Elder Horton said:

— I hope the closing hymn is "God Be With You Till We Meet Again".

— It is – Elder Cleaver answered.

Everybody liked that, it was the perfect (kind of sad) hymn for Goodbyes. We sang and later we gave our business cards to each other. Every missionary received a business card with our information and names, for people get in touch with us after our mission, it was a tradition in our mission (and the cards were called in Japanese "meishi"). One Sister of our district, Sister Robertson, gave us a meishi with a quote in the back that said: "How lucky I am to have a friend that makes saying goodbye so hard" (it is written that it is a quote from

Winnie The Pooh). It was a beautiful quote that made me feel a little better.

I was even surprised with the sadness of a transfer, I should be used to it by now. It is how the mission works, we meet great people and become friends, but eventually we must part ways. But I also think that it makes sense to always feel a little sad when a good friend goes away.

One day, going back to Inuyama, Elder Cleaver fell asleep on the train. After some time, I heard the voice on the train speakers saying that we were arriving at a specific train station. So, I woke up Elder Cleaver and we left on that station (the right one).

— How did you know we were at the right place? – He asked.

— I heard the woman on the train saying – I answered.

— Very good! You are ready to be transferred – He joked. Foreigners usually find it hard to understand what people are saying on the speakers of train stations.

— Thanks – I said with a smile, but I wasn't very excited about transfers.

On Friday night, we received a call from the Zone Leaders telling us that Elder Cleaver was going to be transferred and my new companion would be someone called "Elder Bahr."

— Do you know him? – I asked Elder Cleaver.

— No. But I think I heard about him.

Two days later Elder Bahr called and we talked about how we would meet since missionaries are not supposed to be alone even during transfers, if possible. At some point Elder Bahr said:

— You're Brazilian, right? How is your English?

— It's good – I answered.

— You're fluent. Don't be humble – Elder Cleaver mentioned by my side – He might think that language will be a barrier between you two.

True. I hadn't thought about that.

— Don't worry about my English, it's okay – I said to him.

— Oh, that's good – Apparently, he really was worried about that. Made sense, he knew I was new on the mission field.

Having a new companion would be a new experience and it made me worried and excited at the same time. Amazing how those two emotions are often present during the mission.

11

A New Companion

While Elder Cleaver packed his bags in preparation for his transfer, which would be on Tuesday, I talked with him about the area and made many notes with the names of most members of the ward. It wasn't necessary to make any notes about the people we were teaching because I already knew everything about them, but I really wanted to have details about the ward, the area, and the members.

That day, Elder Kitayama called us and I talked to him for a while. After some time he asked:

— And how do you feel about being area senpai, now?

— Area senpai? – I asked. There usually is a senpai in a companionship, or a senior, as we would say in English.

— Yes. You will be the older missionary in Inuyama – He explained.

— I hadn't thought about that before – I said realizing he was right.

Kitayama laughed a little.

— Don't worry, I'm sure you'll do a great job – He said.

— Thanks – I said also thinking it was funny – But I think it will be fine. I spent a long time asking all the information to Elder Cleaver, so I think I'm ready.

On Tuesday, we woke up very early and went to the Train Station in Nagoya. It was a huge place where many different lines arrived, so it was usually a perfect place to meet with other missionaries. Everybody always agreed to meet at the same place, close to a big golden clock, this way, no missionary would be alone.

There, I started talking to other missionaries, some I had not met before and some I had seen at Zone Conferences. One Elder asked me what I was thinking of Japan and I told him about my travel to get there and about my language studies.

— Wait a second – He said looking confused – So you didn't know any Japanese before coming?

— No.

— Have you ever been to Japan before?

— No.

— How didn't you feel terrified? I would've felt horrible – He said.

I was glad I hadn't met him earlier on my mission, he would have made me nervous. I said goodbye to Cleaver, and after a few minutes, Elder Bahr arrived. He was more or less around my height and had black hair. He was American but was of Japanese descent on his mother's side.

We came back together to Inuyama and that same day I explained to him everything about our area and the people we were teaching. I also explained to him everything about Goku and how well he was progressing.

It took some time for us to get used to each other. Elder Bahr was a good missionary, he wanted to be obedient and had a good heart, but I needed time to get used to some of his habits and personality and I think he felt the same way about me. The same day he arrived we had a lesson with Goku and he met Elder Bahr for the first time.

It was always nice to see Goku and every once in a while we would eat at some restaurant before or after our lessons to have dinner with him. Sometimes brother Fabio joined us. Goku was a good friend and it was always great to meet with him.

Eventually, Elder Bahr and I started to get along better. Our DKKs were a good time for us to talk to each other and I realized that having honest and open conversations was very important to have a good companionship. One thing that we started doing was to watch during our lunch the movie "Legacy" which tells the early history of the church. It was impossible to watch the whole movie during one lunch, it usually took 3 meals to finish the movie, but we watched so many times during that transfer that we would randomly quote the movie to each other during the day. I still know all the lines of the movie to this day.

One day, a member of the church invited us to go play basketball with him and some friends in a town called Mitake. Most of the people who were going to be there were not members of the church, so he thought it was a nice way for them to know the missionaries, and it really was.

I never had been to Mitake, although it was in our area, and neither had Elder Bahr, of course. Our phone was not a smartphone, that is why we had tablets, but with our flip phone (really popular in Japan) we could research train times and destinations. We saw the train that we needed to get and went to Mitake.

We were talking the whole way there and waiting for the right train station. However, the train reached the end and eventually started to return to Inuyama. We left at the same station where we had embarked and were very confused. Had we gotten on the wrong train?

We asked information to a worker at the train station and he explained that we had taken the right train, but we needed to leave the train and take another one, that was from another train line, to reach Mitake. Gladly, people in Japan were always very polite and eager to help. There even are signs in train stations with a drawing of a lost foreigner and a local person offering help. Those signs were always encouraging people to help foreigners who needed assistance. Missionaries always laugh at the signs because they represent us very often.

Both Elder Bahr and I laughed a lot at our stupid mistake and took the same train again. This time we left at the right stop and arrived at Mitake. We were late for the basketball game but were still able to talk with everyone and even play a little.

After playing basketball my knee always hurt a little and it was a sad reminder that I needed to be careful and couldn't run.

An important detail was that Elder Bahr had never seen how bad I was riding a bike, and now I was much better, so we started to go farther with bikes to other nearby cities. I didn't tell him that I was really bad, but I did mention that I had learned with Elder Cleaver, so my skill with the bike was limited.

But my experience of learning recently how to ride a bike was unexpectedly useful. Sister Mac was now training a missionary, her name was Sister Paras and she was Filipina. She had the same problem I had when I arrived at Inuyama, she didn't know how to ride a bike, so Sister Mac asked us if in the afternoon that she would practice, we could help her learn.

I explained to Sister Paras everything that I had recently learned and told her some exercises to practice balance that Elder Cleaver had used to teach me. It worked surprisingly well and she quickly was able to stand on the bike and ride it.

— You are a good teacher – Brother Fabio told me. He was at the parking lot with us.

— Thank you. Who would imagine it would be so useful to learn recently? – I joked.

The season was already getting much more pleasant since it was already September, but it started to rain a lot, and many times the temperature was relatively low, which made the rain a little worse to endure. Usually, my only problem with the rain was that we needed to be careful not to let the water ruin our Books of Mormon or our pamphlets, but now I had another problem, the rain in the cold weather made me very cold by the end of the day, and I also thought that it could make us catch a cold. Unfortunately, I was right about this last part.

One day, brother Endou invited us to go to his house. The Endou family taught Eikaiwa at his house and invited us to be there, helping them to teach and share a spiritual message at the end. That seemed great to us, we went to a town close to Inuyama, did some proselyting there, and then went to the train station. Unfortunately, we were late, so finding a parking place for our bikes was unexpectedly hard. We locked our bikes and left them close to a bathroom surrounded by grass.

It would be fine because we would come back later that same night to get the bikes. The Endou family lived pretty far away. Far enough that going there by bike was not a good option. Once we got to their house, we participated in the class and shared a message. However, they also wanted us to have dinner with them after the class. They were very kind and said we didn't have to worry because they would give us a ride home. Of course, we accepted.

We got to our apartment right before 21:00, exactly when we should. We sat on our chairs to talk about the day and only then did we realize that our bikes were still where we had left them! We were both very worried since that wasn't the right place to park, it was perfectly possible that they wouldn't be there anymore. Not because it would have been stolen, but because the police officers could have taken it from that place (it wasn't a place to park any bike).

If that had happened, we would have had to pay a fee to get it back. The next morning we left very early, took a train, and sat next to the window. It would be possible to see our bikes once we got close to the train station if the bikes were still there, that is. I was looking very closely through the window and saw both bikes.

The relief was amazing.

— The bikes are still there! – I told Elder Bahr.

We were both very happy and relieved. We never again took that train station to go to the Endou's house. There was no parking place next to the train station.

Another typhoon was coming and we received instructions as to when we should be in our apartment. This time the typhoon was coming at night and that was a blessing, we wouldn't be stuck at our apartments for most of the day. However, just like last time, the sky was dark, clouds were moving very fast, and most people were worried and told us to be careful with the typhoon later that day.

We started heading home on our bikes. The rain was pouring. The wind was so strong that I could only hear the noise of it in my ears. I was riding straight home with Elder Bahr on my left side. Suddenly, the wind hit my left side with unbelievable strength. My bike left the ground for a second and hit it again.

— We need to go home! – I screamed very scared at the fact that the wind had just lifted me with the bike.

— I know! – Elder Bahr screamed back, he also seemed scared by the storm – We're almost there!

Yes, we were very close and laughed a lot (of relief) once we got to the apartment. It was probably reckless of us to stay that late outside when we knew that there was a typhoon coming. But Inuyama apparently was at a great place, geographically speaking, because there was never any destruction at the place, thankfully.

Every time there was a typhoon, our mission leaders called us to ask if we were fine. My parents told me later that the Straton couple sent emails to our parents saying that we were safe. My parents loved Elder and Sister Straton because of this kind of thing.

The weather started to become cold. I loved cold weather, so it was no problem for me, I only complained when it was 3°C (37.4 °F) and still raining, that wasn't very pleasant. By the way, it was a big surprise to me that Japan also used Celsius, the same as Brazil, which made things easier for me, but harder for my American companions.

Unfortunately, Elder Bahr became sick. Eventually, I got what he had, but I got healed faster than he did. One night, Elder Bahr was particularly bad and couldn't stop coughing. He was very upset about not being able to work.

— Elder, I think we should go out – Elder Bahr said, still looking pretty sick.

— But Sister Judd told you to rest – I reminded him.

— I'm fine – He said with a smile.

— Ok. If you take a deep breath without coughing, we can go – I said.

He took a deep breath and immediately started to cough. We both laughed and he gave up. Obviously, I wanted to leave and preach the gospel, but he really needed to rest, and I was a little worried about him. I was actually glad Elder Bahr liked to work so much. Being stuck with a companion that didn't want to work was probably horrible.

Eventually, Elder Bahr went to a doctor. There was a person called Niwa who was fluent in English and was always at our Eikaiwa classes, he went to the doctor with us to help translate everything to the doctor. It was a great help.

Eventually, the day of Goku's baptism came. It was a very special day. Elder Cleaver came to Inuyama with his companion and the ward's bishop gave Goku a ride to the church. I don't think it is possible to express in any language the happiness that I felt that day. The children of primary sang a song before his baptism and it was very cute. They started to fight to see who would hold the microphone, but Goku loved that, he thought it was very sweet, and it really was.

Goku shared his testimony after the baptism and expressed how happy he was that he met the missionaries because we had introduced him to the gospel of Jesus Christ. Later, I asked him how he was feeling.

— It's like there's no room in my heart for all the happiness I am feeling – He answered.

I was very happy for him. We kept teaching him the lessons after his baptism and sometimes he would join us at night to preach the gospel. When we met someone who was from Vietnam, he talked a lot with the person and could really connect with them.

Those were very happy days.

12

My First Thanksgiving

It was my second transfer with Elder Bahr and my fourth transfer in Inuyama. It was at this transfer that Goku got baptized and it was already November. Our district leader was Elder Buchanam and his companion was Elder Hamblim.

They set a date with us to have our koukan at Gifu where we would eat together. Coincidently, it was the same day as Thanksgiving, and Elder Buchanan told us that he would like to celebrate it with the three of us.

— Thanksgiving is a big Holiday in the United States, right? – I asked Elder Bahr – Like, it is very important, isn't it?

— It is! – He quickly answered – You don't celebrate Thanksgiving in Brazil?

— No.

— I guess it makes sense. It is a Holliday from the United States – Elder Bahr commented.

— It will be fun to celebrate it for the first time – I said.

We took a train to Gifu the next day. I was starting to get really good at putting my bike on the bike bag, I could take off the front wheel tie it to the side, and put everything inside the bag in less than two minutes. Elder Bahr was also very fast.

Gifu was far more urban than Inuyama, and every time I went there I thought that the Lord had blessed me a lot not sending me there in the beginning of my mission. It was harder to ride a bike there than it was at Inuyama, there were more people on the streets and more objects on the way, even on the sidewalk. Gladly, now it was fine for me.

The place where the Elders lived in Gifu was the best house I had ever seen (for missionaries) on the mission. It was a two-floor house very big and beautiful, but the Elders told me that a bigger house was harder to clean and the two of them could never be on separate floors (missionaries are supposed to be together all the time, so we should always try to be at the same room, or being able to see each other). So, there were pros and cons.

They had bought meat to make a barbecue and had cooked brownies. It was a great meal, and we took a picture to celebrate it. After lunch, we left and I did proselyting with Elder Buchanam and saw he was very funny and had great Japanese. That day we found a family and taught them the gospel, but the family was from Pakistan and the parents couldn't speak Japanese, so their children translated our message for them. It was a great experience.

Now that my Japanese was better, it bothered me more when people were rude to me because I could actually understand how rude they were being. But we all did our best not to be upset or sad about anything that people spoke. For the most part, I was very good at ignoring when people said mean things or were rude.

That same week, I had interviews with President Judd.

— Do you have any questions for me? – President Judd asked me.

— Well, I want to be a good missionary. What do you suggest me to do in order for me to be better? – It was an honest question. President Judd definitely had a lot of wisdom regarding missionary work and I wanted his advice.

— There is something I think every missionary should do – He said calmly – Everyday, before you sleep, during your prayer, you should tell the Lord everything that happened during your day. Tell the Lord everything about your work and ask the Lord if He is happy with your work and what you should do better.

That was a beautiful advice. I immediately felt that that was something I needed to do. Many times in my life, before going on a mission, I had heard experiences of men who had served missions and asked the Lord if He accepted their missions. That always seemed odd to me. What if the answer was "no"? The person wouldn't be able to go back in time and do a better job.

President Judd's advice was an answer to that problem. If I felt every day that the Lord was happy with my work (and worked hard enough to make the Lord satisfied with my efforts), I wouldn't need to ask if the Lord accepted my mission, I would have asked every day already.

And that was valuable advice during my entire mission. Every night I told the Lord everything about my day and on the following day did my best to improve at the points that I felt the Lord wanted me to improve.

The job of a missionary was also to strengthen the ward in which they served and we often served at the Inuyama ward. Many times I taught the lesson to the Brazilian members, when the teacher was not able to go. Sometimes, I also did my best to translate the sacrament meeting to them. Usually, brother Fabio translated (perfectly) to them, but when he was not able to go because of his work, I had to translate.

My Japanese was still not good enough to make an excellent translation so sometimes I listened to the English translation on my left ear and translated from English to the members. It was a great experience and I know that Lord always helped me to translate.

One P-day, Elder Bahr and I found a small mall next to the place where we did groceries. On the second floor, there was one claw machine filled with stuffed Pokémons. We thought it could be fun to try to get one and filmed ourselves trying. After trying three times I was able to get one Pokémon that Elder Bahr told me was called Munchlax (I couldn't remember the name). I tried two other times to get another one but didn't succeed, so I decided to give up and be happy with the one I had.

That was the first and only time I was able to get anything in a claw machine. But Elder Bahr wasn't so lucky. He really wanted a "Charmander" and tried for a long time, but he just couldn't get it.

Eventually, we told the sisters about the claw machine, and in the following week, Sister Mac told us that she got one Pokémon, a "Bulbasaur". Elder Bahr was determined to get a Charmander and for the next three weeks, every P-day, he tried to get his Charmander on that claw machine. After failing he was always sad and said it was a waste of money. I honestly agreed but tried not to laugh or say anything harsh, because he was always very depressed about not getting his Charmander.

I made many jokes about the whole thing the following day, and he also laughed and decided never to look at that machine again. However, on the following P-day, there we were again. And he still was not able to get the Charmander.

At night, when we talked with Elder Buchanan, he talked about how sad it was that he couldn't get it, how frustrating that machine was, and what a waste of his money it was. It came to the point where actually going to a store and buying that Pokémon would've been cheaper. Elder Buchanan was able to get authorization to go to Inuyama (on an authorized day) and went to the claw machine. I have no idea how many times it took for him, but he got the Charmander and gave it to Elder Bahr. We were all very happy, especially Elder Bahr.

This silly experience made me think that Elder Buchanan was a good leader. This was a great example of ministration from Elder Buchanan to Elder Bahr. We should help each other, even on the small things. This had nothing to do with the important job of our mission, but it made Elder Bahr very happy and it wasn't something Buchanan had to do, he just wanted to help a friend and do something nice for him. I think we all should do small acts of kindness to other people, like he did.

As the transfer came to an end, on Friday, we received a call from Elder Buchanan telling us what would happen the next transfer. I would be transferred to a city named Fujieda and my new companion would be Elder Wood. We would be co-senpai (seniors). I actually had heard about that place and that Elder before because that was Elder Orsi's area, and he was companions with Elder Wood. What a funny coincidence.

The next day, on Saturday, we needed to go to Meitou, since the Meitou Stake was going to have an activity for the youth. All the missionaries close to Nagoya needed to go to the Meitou ward (the one next to the Mission Office), and we would spend the day doing missionary work with one or two young men (and the sisters with do the same with young women).

We woke up, got ready for the day, and left our apartment at 5:00 am. The sky was still dark, there was no one on the street, all the stores were closed and above all the buildings there were dozens of crows.

— There are so many crows! – Elder Bahr mentioned being very impressed.

— It's almost like a horror movie – I mentioned with a smile.

— That's what I was thinking!

We arrived at the Meitou ward and President Judd told us that he really wanted the youth to have a great experience, so we should do our best to help them have a good experience and feel the Spirit. We also should avoid talking with the many other missionaries that were there and focus on talking to the members, to encourage them to do missionary work.

Arrangements had already been made. I would be with another missionary (I didn't know who) and with one or two members. I was honestly a little nervous, we were going to do dendou (proselyting) in the Fukutoku area. I loved Fukutoku but had never done any missionary work, besides on my first transfer (and I was a little lost back then). I kind of hoped that the Elder who would be my companion would be someone I knew, which would make planning easier.

My companion would be Elder Silva. He was Brazilian and was on his last week on the mission field. I had never talked much with him, but he was known for being one of the funniest missionaries on the field. I quickly saw that his reputation was well-earned, he was hilarious, especially when he was speaking Portuguese.

— I wish I knew Portuguese just so I could understand what he says – Elder Bahr told me at the end of the day – Every time he speaks you all start crying of laughter.

And there was one 14-year-old young man called Yujinuma who would spend the day with us. He was very nice and a little shy, but we talked with him a lot during the day and walked around Nagoya, in the Fukutoku area.

— Elder Irineu, I'm worried he will have a horrible experience – Elder Silva told me at the beginning of the day.

— Don't worry, it will be fine – I said trying to be optimistic, but also genuinely thought he would probably have some fun. I always thought going out with the missionaries was fun, back home. But I admit it wasn't something I did very often.

— But what if we stop someone and the person starts screaming at us?! – He asked, afraid.

— It probably won't happen – I said. It was rare to find someone very rude, but it did happen sometimes.

— But what if it does?! It could leave him with a bad first impression!

— Maybe we avoid people who look mean – I suggested.

— Great idea! If you see someone that looks angry, don't stop him! – Elder Silva loved the idea.

That would be interesting. My whole mission, so far, I have done my best to talk with everyone I could, no matter the person's appearance or humor. I mean, sometimes we think someone looks angry but looks can be deceiving, so it was best to talk with everyone, no exceptions. But that day we were focused on showing a good experience to the kid. As a matter of fact, President Judd had changed the rule that we could only speak with men during my second transfer, so we could speak with literally anyone. Of course, we were always very respectful with everyone as well.

That day was very cold. Even for people from Nagoya was a day unusually cold. Sadly, Elder Silver had packed most of his clothes and he didn't think the day would be so cold, so he wasn't with coats warm enough. I gave him my gloves, but the day was very cold, so that was the best I could do.

We walked around the city and stopped many people. We told Yuji a few things he could say and invited him to bear his testimony about what we shared with the person. We had lunch at a nice restaurant and talked with a lot of people. Gladly, everyone we stopped was very polite and some people even wanted to hear what we had to say. Yuji gave three pamphlets (following our cues) and shared his testimony about the church.

We took a train to arrive close to the Fukutoku's ward. Elder Silva was worried because he didn't know the way to the church and we ended up being late to the train station since we were not used to the place's geography.

— Don't worry, I know how to get to the church – I assured him.
— Are you sure? – Elder Silver asked.
— Yes – I said with confidence.
— Great.

We left the train station and I guided us through the streets until a staircase that was really close to the church. Yujinuma asked me if I was sure we were on the right track.

— Yes, don't worry, I walked this way a few times – I assured them with a smile.

— I'm not worried, I will just tell people I was following you – Elder Silva joked.

We arrived at the ward and everybody was together to share testimonies and tell how the experience went. Yujinuma shared that he had a great experience and that it was very interesting to see how missionaries spend their days.

— We did it! He had a good experience! – Elder Silva told me with a big smile.

I also smiled and was surprised at how worried Elder Silva really was. Other young men and women shared about their experiences and they all mentioned that they had a new respect for missionaries, because it was really hard, especially since the day was so cold. It really was a great experience, I was glad I've been a part of it.

I came back to Inuyama with Elder Bahr and started packing. Soon I would go to a new area. How different would it be from Inuyama?

I couldn't wait to find out.

13

Lost at The Christmas Concert

Leaving Inuyama was sad, as I expected. It had been my first area and I would miss the members. Many members told me that they were very sad I was leaving and one of them cried. I was very surprised with this member who cried and said he would miss me because I honestly thought he didn't like me very much. I was touched and very happy to see that I was wrong. That was also a gentle reminder to me that we should never assume how someone feels or thinks about anything.

I called the Fujieda Elders to talk with them about how we would meet, but who answered was Elder Orsi. It was really nice to talk with him again, and he explained everything about Fujieda. I also talked with Elder Wood, he and Elder Orsi seemed to get along really well and that was a great sign to me.

— Irineu, you're going to love the train station, it's Christmas there! – He was very excited.

— Really?! – I was surprised. Christmas is not a big Hollyday in Japan, if anything, it's more romantic there. It is a Hollyday to spend with your girlfriend. But something very common there is to eat a "Christmas cake", which I think it's fantastic. Most of them don't know, but Christmas is the birthday of Jesus Christ, so a cake makes perfect sense to me.

— Yes! The train station is filled with lights. You can only see it at night, though – He commented – And the bathroom is amazing!

— The Bathroom? – I laughed a little. The bathroom is not the first part of the house that I would think about.

— You'll see.

— Elder Orsi is helping me to pronounce your name right – Elder Wood said.

I laughed.

— Don't worry about that – I said with sincerity. Elder Cleaver and Bahr had no problem saying "Irineu" with the right intonation, but I never corrected anyone.

On Monday night, Elder Bahr helped me to see which trains I would take to Fujieda. It didn't make sense to meet at Nagoya, since it was in the opposite direction to Fujieda. Fujieda was east, in the Shizuoka prefecture (it was also the Shizuoka zone). I was a little nervous about the trip since it would be my first time taking a train alone.

Elder Bahr noticed that and wrote down on a piece of paper all of the trains and times. It was very kind of him. It was also very safe to write down the times that each train would arrive. Trains are almost never late in Japan, it's amazing.

I said goodbye to Elder Bahr and left with a backpack and my bike on a train heading to Fujieda. Elder Bahr took another train to Meitou. Since he would train someone, he needed to meet other missionaries at the honbu (Mission Office).

My travel went pretty fine up until a train station in the city of Toyohashi. After Toyohashi, it was almost a straight line until Fujieda, but I didn't know that back then. I left the train at the right stop but asked a woman who worked at the train station how to get to Fujieda. She was very kind and helpful, as all Japanese usually are. She showed me which train I should get.

I waited for my train to arrive and saw another train arrive behind me, three Elders left from that train. I had never seen any of them, but we talked to each other, and they asked me where I was going.

— Fujieda. A woman who works here told me that the right train would arrive soon – I explained.

They had come from where I was going, areas above Fujieda, so they knew the way very well.

— Yes, this is your train! – They pointed to the train coming.

I Thanked them and entered the train. It was funny how missionaries didn't need to know each other, we knew that we were from the same mission, so we were automatically friends. Elder Wood had mentioned that I should be careful because the Japan Tokyo South Mission was close to the Shizuoka area's border. So, I should be careful not to leave my Mission by accident.

I arrived at Fujieda and saw two Elders at the train station. One of them was Elder Stanley and the other was Elder Wood. I had met Elder Stanly before, so it was nice to see him again. Elder Wood I had seen in pictures. He was tall and had red hair. There was also a member of the church with them, his name was Toshikazu and he was only a little older than me. He became a very good friend while I was at Fujieda and for the rest of my mission.

I had lunch with Elder Wood and Toshikazu. We ate at a very traditional restaurant where we sat on the floor, next to a small table and ate ramen. It was delicious. After that, we went to our apartment.

The apartment in Fujieda was very good, and it was bigger than the Inuyama apartment, we even had a couch. One of the first things that I wanted to see was the bathroom since Elder Orsin said it was amazing. And it definitely was unique. All of the walls were made of wood and it was very rustic. Inside that bathroom, you felt like you were inside an old hut, in the middle of woods. It was pretty cool, not going to lie.

We had a small DKK where Elder Wood explained to me everything about the area, and we left to buy things for the week. Elder Wood knew how to cook very well and sometimes made a soup that I tried to learn, but was never able to do it right. The next day we met the Sisters of the area. Their names were Sister Clark and Sister Bartholomew.

They were great Sisters. Sister Clark was very funny. I laughed at almost anything she said for the entire time she was at Fujieda. Sister Bartholomew was very kind and very smart, she usually made great comments about the scriptures. Both were very obedient to the mission rules, it was notable.

After talking about the area for some time, Sister Clark told me:

— Your English is very good!

— Thank you!

— Where did you learn? – She asked with a curious look.

— Well, we study English at school, of course. But I mostly learned from watching movies and with "friends" – I explained.

She agreed with a smile, but after a second I realized that my sentence wasn't very clear.

— When I say friends, I mean the TV show "Friends". I used to watch a lot in English – I clarified.

We all laughed.

— That makes more sense. I imagine your friends in Brazil speak Portuguese as well – She said.

— Yes.

Around this time of my mission, I received a package from my family, it was a Christmas gift from them. It was when it hit me that I would spend Christmas far from my family, which could be weird. But Elder Wood loved Christmas, he was the definition of the Christmas Spirit, so it was a great transfer with him. The days felt like a vacation, and not because we were not working (we were working very hard), but because everything was always smooth that transfer, I was never really stressed.

On my first week in Fujieda, the Zone Leaders called us and explained that they would need to go to Meitou, in Nagoya, and would be able to teach Eikaiwa, so they asked us if we could go to Shizuoka and teach the class for them. It wouldn't be a problem for us, because the Sisters could teach Eikaiwa in Fujieda.

We took the keys to their apartment with them at the train station and waited for our train to take us to Shizuoka. While we were watching a huge train passed in front of us very fast. The train was filled with many cargo wagons. It was so fast you almost felt like trying to touch it. Of course, I couldn't do this because it would send me to the hospital.

— This is so cool! – I told Elder Wood while the train was passing.
— Don't jump – He told me.
I laughed a lot.
— How do you know I was thinking about that?
— I think everybody does – He said.

We left for Shizuoka and talked a lot on the way there. Elder Wood and I had similar hobbies, we both watched many of the same movies and we both liked to write, so it was very easy to talk to him.

Once we arrived at Shizuoka, I saw that it was a big city. The train station was beautiful and had many lights on the floor, which made the place amazing to see at night. We ate ramen at a great place and walked to the church, to teach Eikaiwa.

There was only one problem, we couldn't be in different rooms to teach two classes. But solving this was easier than I thought, we just closed the wall in the middle of the room (the room was made in a way that it could be divided in two, closing a wall in the middle). I taught alone the advanced class, and it was very fun.

I noticed that I had progressed a lot already on my mission. At the beginning of my mission, I would have felt nervous teaching alone, but now I was used to it. We slept in the apartment of the Shizuoka Elders.

The next morning we left very early and very fast. There was a service project in Fujieda and a member had asked for our help. But, on the way to the train station, I saw Mount Fuji in the distance, it was very cool. We arrived at our apartment, changed our clothes (because it would be hard to use our white shirts and ties for that activity), and went to the church to wait for the members.

The church building in Fujieda was very interesting. Fujieda was a branch and the place that the church rented used to be a karaoke, so it was a three-store, pink building. The church only really used two floors because the third one was an empty apartment. I really liked that building, it was different and pink on the outside, but on the inside, it was exactly like a regular church building.

Back home, in Porto Alegre, there was a church building that had a light shade of green. So, the different colors made me remember home in a way. Brother Kimura arrived at the church with his car and gave us a ride to a mountain filled with oranges, apparently, we would help the members to get oranges.

They gave Elder Wood and me some specific-shaped scissors and we used them to collect the oranges. It was pretty fun. Close to midday, brother Kimura took us back to the church where we took our bikes and went back home to plan the rest of the day.

On Sunday, we went to the house of a member called brother Lorenzo. He was from Peru and was a very kind person with a lot of faith. He really wanted the missionaries to eat lunch at his house every Sunday after church. We, the Sisters and two other members went to his house, ate, and then we shared a message with him.

Brother Lorenzo didn't know many words in Japanese and didn't know any English, so I had to translate everything for him. It was great to talk to him. His native language was Spanish, but he did know some Portuguese and I can understand Spanish, as long the person speaks slowly. Brother Lorenzo gave us so much food that I gained weight while I was in Fujieda.

The next day was P-day and we needed to go to Meitou. Apparently, there was going to be a "Japan Nagoya Mission Christmas Concert", and Elder Wood was going to sing in the choir. We took a train and went to Nagoya. Since Fujieda was really far from Nagoya, we would sleep in the house of the Elders from Okazaki. The Elders there were Elder Yamada and Elder Gardanier. Elder Gardanier had been my district leader when Elder Bahr became my companion, so we knew each other well.

The day (actually, it was night) was really fun and I saw Elder Orsi, Cavalcanti, and Sister Galdino again. After Elder Wood finished practicing, we went to the Okada train station and slept in the apartment there (it was the Okazaki area).

The next day, I woke up feeling great and had no idea it would be one of the most stressful days of my mission. We left with the other Elders and arrived at the Meitou church building at 8:30 am. We had a Zone Conference and it was great.

Since it was December, the Zone Conference was focused on the Savior Jesus Christ. President and Sister Judd talked about how the Savior is the real focus of Christmas, and how we celebrate His birth. The Plan of Salvation is only possible because of Him and His atoning Sacrifice.

After the Zone Conference and the rehearsal for the Concert, we decided to have dinner, since we wouldn't have time later. Elder Orsi, Cavalcanti, and many other missionaries were with us. On the way there, Elder Wood said:

— I need to stop at a convenience store. Is that ok?

— Of course – I said.

— But we won't have time to eat – Elder Orsi said – Why do you need to go?

— Because I haven't picked up my money for this transfer. I'm using my "White Mon" – Elder Wood said – And I have money, I just didn't have time to pick up it yet.

— No, no, no. You can go take your money after the Concert, now we need to eat! – Orsi said in a hurry.

Elder Wood looked at me.

— Getting your money is important, so we can go if you want. But you can choose – I said. It didn't seem very important, we could go to a convenience store after the concert.

— Let's go eat – He said.

We went to a Chinese restaurant and had a great dinner. After that, we had to go running to the church. Since I was not going to sing, I tried to be useful in other ways. I became companions with Elder Salzl for some time and we invited people on the street to enter the church and hear beautiful hymns about the Savior. After some time, we went to the church and greeted people who were coming in.

Elder Orsi came to me and asked if he could put his tablet in my bag.

— I don't think it's a good idea – I said with a bad feeling.

— I will take it back after the concert! – He said.

— Why can't you put on your bag? – I asked.

— It's on the second floor and I don't have my companion with me – He explained.

— It would be easy to lose your tablet or something like that – I argued. For some reason, I felt that wasn't a good idea.

— Stop being silly, Irineu – He said with a smile.

— Okay, sure – I agreed. I put his tablet in my bag.

After that, I kept helping organize the place and guiding people to the room where they could sit. I saw many people from Inuyama there, including Goku. He went there with Elder Bahr and his new companion, Elder Coelho, a Brazilian missionary. The concert was beautiful and we could feel the Spirit there.

After the concert ended I said goodbye to many people, including Elder Orsi, Cavalcanti, Bahr, and others. Elder Wood and I walked to the train station and started going to the Nagoya train station.

Suddenly, I felt our phone ringing. I answered and saw it was Elder Orsi.

— Irineu, you have my tablet – He said a little worried.

— Oh no! – I became worried very quickly.

That was horrible! It was exactly for that that I didn't want to have his tablet. How could I have forgotten?! Our tablet was very important for missionary work. It had an app called "area book" where we kept our schedule, notes about our lessons, and even had a map of our areas.

— Where are you? – He asked.

It wasn't polite to talk on the phone on a train, but I would have to be rude in that situation.

— We're going to Nagoya – I said and turned to Elder Wood – Elder Orsi's tablet is in my bag.

— Oh no! – Wood said immediately understanding the situation.

— We could wait in Nagoya for you, but only if you're already going there. It's almost 22:30 and we can't wait any longer – I said.

— I'm already on the train – Elder Orsi assured.

— Are you sure? – I asked, it felt like a lie.

— Well, I'm at the train station – He corrected.

— I could leave your tablet with the Elders of Okada and they could give it to the Assistants – I suggested. The assistants could give the tablet to Elder Orsi. Wood was listening to the conversation.

— No! My area is really far! – Orsi said – Just wait for me in the Nagoya station!

— Wood, what should we do? – I asked. It was partially my fault that we were in that situation, so I really wanted to follow his decision.

— Give me the phone – He asked – Orsi, are you already at the train station? Are you sure? Ok.

We decided to wait for him at the train station. The Okada Elders parted from us and took the train to Okada. Elder Wood and I waited for a long time in the street, in front of the place where our train would leave. After 30 minutes, it became clear Orsi was lying, and he was probably at the Meitou church when we were talking. Elder Wood became very stressed and so did I.

— I'm so sorry, Wood – I said.

— It's fine, Orsi was the one who lied. I'll call him and say we're leaving – Wood took the phone.

While he was calling, Elder Orsi arrived. We gave him the tablet (almost threw it at him) and ran as fast as we could to take the last train to Okada. The train was already leaving, but Elder Wood jumped through the door and I followed him right before the doors closed behind me.

— We did it! – I said very tired and happy.

He was also with a big smile. It was already past 22:30 pm. (at 22:30 the missionaries needed to be with the lights off and at least trying to sleep). After some minutes, Elder Wood became uneasy, saying that something was off. He didn't recognize the stops. I had a bad feeling as well and once the train stopped, I went to someone who worked there and said:

— Excuse me, is this train going to Okada?

He looked at me with a terrified face and said:

— No! You need to leave the train right now!

I turned to my companion:

— Wood!

He left the train and walked toward us. The man said that soon it would be too late and all the trains would stop. He pointed to the other side of the train station and told us to take the first train that passed, we were going in the opposite direction to Okada.

Elder Wood and I followed his instructions and waited for the train. Our phone was almost without any battery and we started to be very stressed.

— Irineu, check on your tablet how far we are from Okada – Elder Wood asked.

I did that and saw that we were 3 hours away from there (walking). With this new information, we became even more worried and Elder Wood started to panicking. He called the Okada Elders, but it didn't even ring, their phone was probably already without any battery.

The train arrived and we entered. We were the only passengers, that only made us more desperate. I started laughing and Wood looked at me a little angry:

— What are you laughing at?

— I'm sorry, but when I'm really nervous, I laugh – I explained.

He started calling every contact we had and no one answered.

— Of course no one is answering! It's almost 23:30! Everyone is sleeping! – He said desperate – I'm going to kill Orsi!

— President Judd will answer! – I said. Now I think it was the Spirit who told me that.

Elder Wood called and I was right, he answered. Wood explained the whole situation to President Judd and told him that we didn't even know where we were (in which city). I couldn't hear what President Judd was saying, but apparently, he told us to take a Taxi.

— Taxis are really expensive, and I don't have any money – Then he looked really stressed and said – I don't have my White Mon.

Oh no.

— I have it! I have it! – I told him.

— Elder Irineu has it! – Elder Wood seemed very relieved.

He closed the phone and looked horrible.

— What happened, what did President Judd say?

— He said we should take a taxi – He answered looking sad.

— What did he say when you told him you don't have a White Mon? – I asked a little worried.

— He said "It's for this type of situation that we keep the White Moon, Elder Wood" – He rested his face on his hands – This is all Elder Orsi's fault, I would have my White Mon, but he convinced me to go eat!

— It's true – I said and laughed feeling very nervous.

Our train arrived at its last stop and we left. It was after 23:30 and no other train would work until the morning. We walked around the empty train station and tried to ask for information, but people were being surprisingly rude to us.

— Why are people being so rude? – I asked Elder Wood surprised.

— It's just our luck – He said.

We talked to a worker that gave us instructions, but was pretty rude and left us.

— Why is this happening?! – Wood asked. Japanese were never rude, but that night was the exception.

But the man told us that leaving the train station, turning right, there was a place where we could ask for a taxi. Our phone had no battery anymore, so we were alone to solve the problem.

We walked on the dark empty street and saw a taxi across the street.

— There! – We said at the same time and started running.

— Yes! – I said very happy.

But exactly at that moment, a woman arrived out of nowhere and entered the car.

— No! – I screamed (completely caused by despair).

Elder Wood ran really fast and reached the window of the car, where the driver was.

— I need to talk to you! – He said looking serious and desperate at the same time.

— I have a passenger! – The man said.

— No! Stop this car and open the door! – Elder Wood said.

— Wood, are you crazy?! – I said. The man would think we were criminals and would call the police.

— Open this door! – Wood commanded.

The driver stepped on the accelerator and got away really fast.

— NO! – Elder Wood screamed.

I started to think the police cars would arrive at any second. Two crazy young men were screaming at taxi drivers, that couldn't be good. I looked around and saw a small house. It was an interesting construction and seemed to be a place to wait for taxis.

— We should go there. Maybe this is a place where taxis stay – I suggested.

— Sure – Wood said looking sad and tired.

We crossed the street and entered the house. It looked like a small office. On the left side, there were some tables. On the right side, there were some chairs and a huge map on the wall which I imagine was a map of the city where we were. On one of the tables, there was a big old telephone and a piece of paper with some numbers.

— I think we can call the taxi place with this – Elder Wood said.

He used the phone to call one of the numbers and talked with someone.

— The woman said they are sending someone here – Wood told me and sat on one of the chairs – I'm actually glad you can laugh at this situation, Irineu, it helps a little.

— Here, let's take a picture – I said and took a picture with my tablet.

Elder Wood looked at the camera, but didn't smile at all.

— Why are you taking a picture?

— Right now, this sucks, but it will be a great story someday – I said trying to make him feel better.

— I don't want to remember anything about tonight – Wood answered – I can't believe I didn't have my White Mon! President Judd must be so disappointed with me!

— What? Don't say that. He's probably glad someone has, and we will be able to go home. I'm sure he is not disappointed with you.

He didn't say anything.

— I'm sorry about this situation – I said again, feeling pretty bad.

— I don't blame you.

— Just Elder Orsi?

— Exactly – He said and I laughed a lot.

After some time, a taxi arrived and took us to the train station of Okada. We didn't know the exact address of the missionaries, but we knew how to get there from the train station. On the way there we didn't talk much. Normally we would talk to the taxi driver about the gospel, but we were both exhausted.

We did mention that we were missionaries of the Church of Jesus Christ of Latter-Day Saints and gave him a meishi with the information about the church. The ride cost a little over 5.000 yen. After that, we arrived at the house and knocked on the door. Elder Gardanier and Yamada were waiting for us. It was 40 minutes after midnight, and their phone didn't have any battery, like ours, so they were just waiting for a long time.

I'm really grateful for the faith they had that we were able to get there, but Elder Yamada did say that thought maybe would have to sleep on the streets. I'm pretty sure he was joking though.

The next morning we woke up at 6:30 very tired, but Elder Wood and I really wanted to get to our house as soon as possible. The missionaries from Okazaki had forgotten their phone charger at the church, so we were not able to call President Judd. That made me feel horrible, he had no idea how we were or if we had arrived at the Okazaki apartment. On the train heading to Fujieda, we had the idea of sending a message using "Line" on our tablet.

We got to our place, charged the phone and Elder Wood called. He really wanted to be the one to talk to President Judd. He explained that we were fine and apologized for not calling before and explained that we didn't have our charger. President Judd didn't seem to be angry, he only wanted to know if we were OK.

Now that I think about it, I think that we should have used the Elders' bikes to get to the church building and charge the phone. But back then I didn't have this idea, none of us did.

— This is horrible, Irineu. I feel so bad.

— Don't worry, Wood – I said trying to comfort him.

— I will forever be the "missionary that didn't have the white mon." I'm sure everybody on our mission will hear this story – He said with a depressed look.

— What? I'm sure no one will know.

— This is the perfect story to tell missionaries to illustrate the importance of the White Mon – Elder Wood said a little upset.

— I guess it is – I had to agree – But I am certain President Judd will not mention our names.

I actually was completely certain of that.

— It's not bad for you, you had the White Mon – Elder Wood joked – This was all caused by Elder Orsi. He stopped me from getting the White Mon, gave you his tablet, forgot the tablet was in your bag, and lied about being at the train station!

I started laughing at that. Weirdly, it was true. Later that day, Orsi called us and apologized. We both forgave him. All of that happened on December 18th of 2018.

14

Shougatsu

The next Sunday was December 23rd and the Fujieda branch wanted the missionaries to prepare a message and one of us to give a talk during sacrament meeting. We went to the church and met with the Sisters. There, we prepared a talk. I suggested that we used a scripture from Iseah that is also present in 2 Nephi talking about the birth of the Savior to finish. They loved the idea, and I opened the scriptures to search for the exact reference.

— Let's do "Rock, Paper, scissors" to decide – I heard one of them saying.

I was too focused on finding the right scripture, so didn't pay attention to what we were deciding, but I won.

— Cool, so what did I win? – I asked.

— You will give the talk on Sunday – Elder Wood answered.

— I see – I wasn't very excited about it.

They all laughed. But it wasn't a problem. I had given talks in Japanese before (even in the MTC, once), but I was usually translating for the members, so on my entire mission, I usually translated for the members who were listening or translated to Japanese on the stand.

We prepared the talk together, so it really wasn't hard to talk about Christmas and the Savior. At the same sacrament meeting the Sisters also sang a Christmas hymn that was beautiful, they were great singers. The next day was Christmas Eve, and the members gave us many Christmas presents.

My knee was hurting, probably because I had run a lot in the last couple of days. I explained to Elder Wood that it would be better for us not to run and started to put ice on my knee every night. It worked.

On Christmas day, our entire District celebrated Christmas together and we had lunch at the church. Our district leader was Elder Gish, and he was a great district leader. Actually, I think he was a great leader in general. He was very good at inspiring us to be better and to work hard, some mission leaders could be a little pretentious or not completely honest about caring about the other missionaries, but Elder Gish was a kind person and a great Elder. We all could see that he applied the things that he asked us to do. He also spoke Japanese really well.

Later that same Christmas, we left with some members of the church to sing at rest houses, hospitals, and asylums. It was really fun to sing Christmas hymns and songs. I had a rattle full of bells and used them while we were singing. It was very fun.

The next day was Christmas for my family, so I could call them using Skype. It was so nice to see everybody again, even my dog Tobby (he was a black shi-tzu). I told everybody how I had spent my Christmas day and they told me how they had spent theirs, since it was 11:00 am for me, but 11:00 pm. for them.

The week of New Year ("shougatsu" in Japanese) is very special in Japan. They are very hard-working people and don't have many Holidays during the Year, so the first week of the year is a Holiday and a time to spend with their families. Because of that, it would be extremely rude to preach the gospel during those days. It would even be pretty bad for the church's image since we would not be respecting the precious time that they can spend with their families.

Since we could not do missionary work, the Mission Office told us many activities that we should do during that week, including a very thorough cleaning of our apartment. But we were allowed to go out with the members if they invited us.

So, on the first day of 2019, Elder Wood and I woke up really early to go with some Eikaiwa students to the top of a mountain to see the first sunrise of the year (it is tradition there). It was very cold, so cold that all the cars on the street had some ice on top of it.

It was a great experience and really fun. Later that week, a member, sister Shimizu, called us inviting us for dinner with her entire family and the Sisters would be there too. I talked to her, and she told me the time to be there. After hanging up, I told Elder Wood.

— You can call her to see if I understood well the time – I suggested.

— No, it's ok – He said calmly.

— Are you sure? What if I didn't understand the time well? – I was afraid of us being late because of me.

— Elder, you have great Japanese, I trust you – Elder Wood said.

I was grateful for his trust, and for the compliment, but was a little worried about the time. She lived very far away, and taking the bike in the cold could be challenging since the wind against us made the temperature feel even colder. The wind in Japan was also very cold, so if I didn't wear gloves while riding the bike, my hand skin would become very dry and start bleeding while I was driving. I love could weather, but it can be pretty challenging while riding a bike.

We arrived at the right time and had a great dinner with the members. They were all very kind and gave us traditional mochi to eat. Mochi is a food made of rice that is traditionally eaten on shougatsu.

When the week ended, I was very happy to go back to do some dendou (proselyting). We had shared messages with the members and casually asked their families if they knew people we could teach, but it was not the same as going out and preaching the gospel.

Eventually, we went to Hamamatsu to do our koukan. Elder Wood would spend the day with Elder Gish and I would spend the day with Elder Gunter, who Elder Gish was training. It was a great day

15

The Prophet Answers My Prayer

I went to the train station and said goodbye to Elder Wood and Sister Clark. It was always sad when a transfer ended and my companion went away, but it was also a good sign. Missing my companions meant that they were good companions.

I stayed in Fujieda with Elder Santos and Elder Bennet, who went to Fujieda to stay with me since the three of us didn't have companions yet. Elder Inagaki was coming to Fujieda, so I just needed to wait for him.

The three of us went to my apartment and started to prepare lunch. Elder Santos was not feeling well, he had a cold. So, he laid down for some time while Elder Bennet and I started to prepare lunch. Unfortunately, we didn't have much in the house, I would buy food later with Elder Inagaki. After thinking for some time, we decided to cook pasta. It was easy and simple. The only problem is that we didn't have a sauce to cook the meat with it.

— We could use "Cook-do" – Elder Bennet suggested.

I had to think for a second. Cook-do was a type of sauce that we used to cook with meat and some vegetables, it was not supposed to be eaten with pasta, but rice. Elder Bennet was known for eating strange combinations, but I admit I was curious to taste that strange combination. Also, we didn't have a lot of food anyway.

— Sure, let's try it! – I agreed.

We made the food and woke up Elder Santos. The three of us sat on the table and started to eat.

— This tastes so... different – Elder Santos said carefully – What is it?

— We used Cook Do with the pasta – I explained with a smile.

— Cook-Do? – He asked me very surprised. Then, he turned to Elder Bennet – I wonder whose idea that was!

We all laughed, but it wasn't so bad. Kind of tasted like soup. Definitely weird, but not bad.

Elder Inagaki arrived later that afternoon and the other two Elders left. We bought food for the apartment and started our DKK, where I explained the area to him. He was Brazilian, like me, but was fluent in English and his Japanese was just as good. We decided that we wouldn't speak Portuguese with one another because we really wanted to practice Japanese and English, especially Japanese in my case.

I really wanted to improve my Japanese, because I felt it could be much better. Elder Inagaki told me that he didn't know how to cook at all, so he would be happy washing the dishes. That was when I realized that I knew how to cook. It was amazing! When I arrived at the mission, I couldn't cook anything, but now I was cooking every day. I even learned to cook new dishes but was never able to replicate the soup that Elder Wood tried to teach me.

The first time we went to the train station was really funny. One of the big trains with many cargo wagons was passing really fast in front of us.

-Wow. This is so cool! – Elder Inagaki said out loud.

-Don't jump – I said smiling.

-I really was thinking about that! – He said very surprised and we both laughed.

Elder Wood was right, everyone thought about that being that close to the train.

Unfortunately, Inagaki got really sick after one or two weeks, and not too long after I got what he had, but after a few days we were better and always did our best to keep working hard. We were actually teaching many people. Among the people who we were teaching there were Japanese, Filipinos, and others, but I never found any Brazilian to teach in Fujieda.

One day, we were feeling better, but not healed. Still, we went to brother Lorenzo's house and I shared a message with him and sister Toshiko. I felt inspired to share a message about Alma chapter 32 in the Book of Mormon which speaks about faith and humility.

At the end of the message, sister Toshiko cried and told me that my message had been very similar to one in the Liahona of that month. She said I had spoken exactly what she needed to hear and thanked me. I was surprised with how I had felt an inspiration to help someone and hadn't noticed.

It is such an amazing and profound feeling when you realize you were used as a tool in the Lord's hand to help someone. I don't think that that is a better feeling.

On P-day, none of us was feeling better. Elder Inagaki had a fever and I was very nauseated. Sister Judd told us to rest that day and we did that after doing groceries. I hated the feeling of staying home and prayed a lot for the Lord to cure us both.

That week, we did another koukan with the Hamamatsu Elders. I went proselyting and, at night, I asked Elder Gunter for a priesthood blessing. His blessing was beautiful and after that day I started to feel better. I also gave Elder Inagaki a blessing and he told me that he felt much better after. Soon after that we were both healed.

The following P-day was very hard. I was talking with my family, through messages, as we always did, and President Judd called me. I got very nervous, why was he calling me himself?

I answered the phone and he told me that my parents had asked if they could call me, and he had allowed it.

— Are you sure it's my parents? – I asked. They were talking to me and everything seemed to be fine.

— Are your parents Domingos and Anna?

— Yes – I suddenly became worried.

— Yes, you can call them.

After that I got afraid, and Elder Inagaki seemed worried as well. I called my parents, and they told me that they had difficult news for me. My brother was going through some serious problems and had divorced his wife, who was a dear friend of mine as well.

They explained the whole problem and I cried. My whole life I had been very close to my family, especially my brother, so that news was very painful. My parents knew that it would be hard for me to know everything and wanted to tell me before I heard from somebody else. They sent an email to President Judd explaining the situation and asking if they could call me.

President Judd was very wise, kind, and thoughtful and allowed the call. After I finished talking to my parents, Elder Inagaki gave me a hug. I think he felt very bad for me and was very supportive from that moment forward with me.

That was a hard day and I prayed a lot during that week and also in the following weeks. The next day I went to Elder Inagaki and told him that he didn't need to worry about me being too sad to work. I would be a great missionary and would work as hard as I could. It would be good for me to be occupied every day and focus on the Lord and on the people we were teaching. I explained all of that to Elder Inagaki and said he didn't need to worry.

He was very kind after that and we started to get along much better after that moment. I am glad he was so supportive.

— I have to say, Irineu, I am sorry about your brother and everything, but I am so grateful it wasn't something worse. When President Judd called, I thought someone had died – He said with a smile.

I laughed.

— Yes, I was a little relieved it wasn't something worse as well – I had to agree.

The night of P-day, the same day I got the news, we were doing some proselyting and two police officers stopped us and asked some questions. Police officers were always very kind in Japan, but they said someone had called and said that there were two foreigners walking around, that's why they were looking for us.

The whole thing seemed silly, and I just didn't have the mood for that, so I didn't worry much. Elder Inagaki got very worried, but the police officers said we weren't doing anything illegal (as I knew we weren't), so we shouldn't worry.

The rest of the week passed fast, but I was still very sad. I knew my parents were also very sad, as well as my sister, who was living very far away with her husband. I wished I could talk to them again to help in any way I could. I prayed about it and asked the Lord to bless my family in any way He could, especially my brother.

I worked hard to focus on my missionary work. There was nothing I could do to help more my family, but I knew the Lord would bless them, and I knew the Lord had called me to be a missionary, so I would work hard.

On Saturday, February 16th, I received an email from the church. The Quorum of Twelve Apostles had made a statement that (on the missions where it was possible) the missionaries were allowed to talk with their families through video calls every P-day or very often.

It was amazing! I was speechless. It was the answer to my prayers, and it was so good that it was hard to believe, almost too good to be true. The Prophet (and all of the apostles) had just changed a big rule at the moment I needed the most. I had no doubt the church was guided by the Lord and revelation was real. I wish I could Thank President Russel M. Nelson for that. He doesn't know what a huge blessing that was for my family and me.

President Judd also sent a message to all missionaries saying that we would follow the Prophet's and the Apostle's command and on P-day we could call our families. That was a great blessing, I was able to talk with my family and share the missionary experiences I was having.

I shared with them everything I was learning on the mission, and I think it helped all of us to strengthen our faith and testimony. I also received a lot of support from missionaries such as my companion and Elder Gish.

Sometimes I called Gish and talked with him. He always listened to me, gave me good advice, and just listened when I was sad. As I said before, he was a good mission leader. On our koukan I explained most of what had happened to my brother (something I mostly kept to myself) and he had many kind words that helped me.

But, I kept working hard with Elder Inagaki and we were teaching many lessons every day. One night, after we left a house (taught a lesson) I saw that it was raining violently hard, so hard that it made me worried. I didn't say anything to Elder Inagaki, we needed to go home, so there wasn't any choice, we had to ride our bikes in the rain.

However, I said a silent prayer and asked the Lord to protect us and make the rain become lighter. The rain immediately became very faint. We rode our bikes and, in the same second we stepped inside our apartment, the rain came back as violently as before.

I was impressed and grateful. The Lord really was listening to my prayers, I was completely certain of that.

16

Fukuroi

My sixth transfer came to an end, and I received news I would be transferred to Fukuroi, to be companions with Elder Nichols. I knew him but had never talked much to him, Fukuroi was in the same district as Fujieda, it was the exact area beneath Fujieda. It would be a quick trip.

I called the mail company and sent my luggage to Fukuroi on Monday and on Tuesday I went to the train station and met Nichols there. He was American, had dark hair, and was my height. He was very happy, outgoing, and overall, a fun person to be around.

We talked on our way to Fukuroi, left the train, walked to a big set of stairs, and walked to our right side. The train station was very beautiful, it had many dolls with traditional Japanese outfits, kind like puppets that would be used to present a show. There was a big escalator and we took it to leave the train station. The day was very bright and sunny, and the city was beautiful.

— Welcome to Fukuroi, Elder Irineu – Nichols said in a dramatic way with a big smile – There is a big parking lot for bikes very close that belongs to the train station, we keep our bikes here.

— How useful – And it really would be.

Elder Nichols got his bike, and I followed him toward our apartment. The city had big streets and after crossing a very long bridge, that was above a big river, we were very close to the church. The church in Fukuroi was a branch, but the church building was very nice. It had one floor, but it was big and had a nice parking lot. The design reminded me of many church buildings in Brazil.

Our apartment was very close to the church, we could just walk there, and it would be fast. We arrived at an orange building and walked to one of the doors. Nichols opened the door and I saw a big staircase in front of me. The door was on the first floor, but the apartment was on the second, which made me laugh a little, I was not expecting to see stairs once I opened the door.

The apartment was very nice. The best I had lived up to that moment. It had a room for us to study, where there was a closet that Elder Nichols was using, the kitchen, the living room (which was really big), and the bedroom with the futons that we used to sleep in. In the bedroom, there was my new closet. In the hallway, after going upstairs there was also one door with the toilet and one door with the sink and shower (and also the bathtub that I don't think anyone ever used).

Elder Nichols and I left to buy groceries and after we came back home, my luggage arrived by mail. So, I unpacked most of my things while Elder Nichols cooked lunch. After that, we went to the church where he explained the area to me.

Fukuroi was a big area. Looking at the map, there was a city on our left that was called Iwata, on our right there was "Aino" (which was a very small and beautiful city, everything there looked very new because everything had been built recently), passing Aino we would arrive at Kakegawa, and then Kikugawa. This last one, Kikugawa was too far to get by bike. Every time we wanted to do some dendou there, we needed to take a train. There were other places, but those were the main big cities that we used as references.

That transfer was very fun, and a big part of this was because of Elder Nichols. He was obedient to all mission rules but was crazy (in a good way). He was a little reckless while riding a bike during our daily travels around the Fukuroi area. After I told him that I had learned how to ride a bike on my mission, he always wanted me to do crazy maneuvers with the bike.

But he was also very intelligent and sometimes had good pieces of advice. One day, we were walking to the train station and talking about another Elder whom Nichols hadn't met yet. I was saying that he was a good missionary and was learning Japanese really fast.

— His Japanese is better than mine and he has less time on the mission – I mentioned.

— Don't do that. Don't compare yourself with others – He said calmly.

— I'm not saying that my Japanese is bad or anything like that... — I started to explain.

— I know. But comparing ourselves to others only makes us sad and doesn't help anyone – He explained.

He was completely right. And I gave that same advice to others for the rest of my mission.

On another day, Elder Nichols told me that he had an allergy in his right eye. While we were walking on the streets, he turned to me and said:

— Is my eye weird?

I looked at his eye and got scared. It was very weird. It was almost as if the white part of his eye was swollen. I controlled my reaction and calmly said:

— It's not that bad. I'm sure it's nothing – I waited a few seconds before continuing – Do you have something to put on your eye?

— Yes, I have some eye drops.

— You should use it – I said.

He did and we kept walking and talking to people on the streets for a while. Then, I walked in his direction.

— Let me see your eye.

— Why? – He asked.

— I want to see if the drops worked – I explained naturally.

I looked at his eye and saw that it was normal now. I immediately felt very relieved.

— Oh good! It's normal now! – I said with a big smile.

— What?! Was it that bad before? – He was surprised by my reaction.

— Yes! It was very weird, but it's Okay now – I told him – I didn't want to make you worried.

He laughed and I remembered when Elder Cleaver told me something similar when my eye was swollen.

The days in Fukuroi were very nice, we had many people to teach and did our best to talk with everyone we could see on the street, which helped me to see many miracles during those days. The members of the church in Fukuroi also were great. The branch president was brother Koide and he asked me two things as soon as he saw me: to translate for the Brazilian members and to give a talk the following week.

There was a very interesting and modern device that the churches use in Japan with two boxes. One of the boxes has a tiny microphone where the translator speaks and the other box is where you plug in the earphones that the members used to hear my voice. After some time, I got better at translating while the speaker gave his (or hers) talk. I had done that before at Inuyama, but my Japanese was much worse at Inuyama.

I started feeling my Japanese was getting better and I was able to speak everything I wanted to say. The Lord was also blessing me so that I could understand the language much better. That was a feeling that I had but didn't mention to anyone.

One day, the Sisters from Fujieda came to Fukuroi for our DTM (District Training Meeting) which while I was at Fukuroi had the name switched to DCM (District Council Meeting). It was Sister Bartholomew and Sister Furutani, who was Japanese.

We, including the Elders from Hamamatsu and Fujieda, talked a lot about missionary work and how to improve. At the end of the meeting, while everyone was getting ready to go home, Sister Furutani came to me and said:

— Elder Irineu, your Japanese is so much better. Good work!

— Really? Thank you! – I said with a big smile.

That compliment made me happy for many days. Sister Furutani was very kind and a great Sister, but that comment was honest, I could tell, and also encouraged me to keep studying the language.

The branch also had many Brazilian members, like the Landin family, they were a family of 5. One of the three siblings was on his mission and the other siblings were very nice and talked to us often. They sometimes bought us and brought delicious foods that they bought at "Costco". Sometimes we went with the two siblings to go bowling on our P-day. All of them helped us with missionary work.

There was also another great family, made up of two parents and two small kids, who were also Brazilian and were very nice to us. They were always very happy and helped us to find more people to teach. Those two families were always willing to help us teach other people. Brother Landin had a great knowledge of the scriptures, especially The Bible, so it was always interesting to talk to him.

There were many other members in Fukuroi who helped us. Our ward mission leader was called brother Matsui. He had a wife and a small child. They were all very sweet and were always willing to help.

One day I was doing a koukan with Elder Cruz, a missionary from Hamamatsu companions of Elder Gish. We found a neighborhood in Fukuroi that had many Brazilians living in it. We knocked on some doors and found a family that had met the missionaries before, they had a lot of faith in their religion, but apparently, they had been taught by the missionaries for a long time.

We talked with them and shared a message. After our lesson, we were talking to them and I looked at the clock. It was close to 21:00 pm, so we needed to go home quickly. The wife noticed that I looked at my clock and told me that she was always impressed and touched by the missionary's obedience to the rules.

— It's just so amazing, because you're all so young, but are so responsible – She said with an honest expression – The missionaries that we met before explained to us that you had time to be back home and they were always so obedient, just like you! I talked to a friend about this, and she told me something that is true, she said: They are not obedient to their rules, they are obedient to God, and that is why they follow the rules.

— Your friend is very wise, sister – I said with a smile – It's true.

I was impressed with how other people noticed our example. I was also very grateful that previous Elders were obedient and set a good example for that family. Even a rule that many may consider not very important is important and exists for a reason.

After that day, I went to that neighborhood again with Elder Nichols. We found another family. They had their own religion, but the wife and husband were having a problem with their own faith. Apparently, in their religion, they didn't believe in life after death and thought that was weird, because they felt that they needed to be with their children after this life.

We sat with them, read the scriptures, and I explained that we believe in Eternal Families. It is possible for us to live forever with our family, not only our children, but our parents, grandparents, and everyone connected to us, everyone that we love. During that lesson, I realized what a great blessing it is to know the Plan of Salvation.

After much conversation, I gave them a Book of Mormon.

— If you pray with faith, the Lord will tell you if this book is true, and I testify that I already prayed and he answered me that it is true. It is the word of God – I told them with sincerity.

— But what if the Lord doesn't answer my prayer? – The wife asked.

— He will – I told her.

— But what if He doesn't? – She insisted. I could see the anguish in her eyes.

— I promise you that He will! – I said looking her in the eyes.

She was speechless for a second.

— It's been a long time since I met someone with so much faith – She told me.

I felt very touched by her comment. I was speaking with my heart and everyone in that room was feeling the Spirit. I could tell. And it is true, everyone who prays to know if the Book of Mormon is true, with faith and honesty, will receive an answer through the Holy Ghost. I know that this is true.

Unfortunately, friends of that family told them lies about the church and they refused to meet us again. Still, I know that they felt that our words were true and they felt very happy to know that our families are eternal. I hope that one day, they will hear the gospel again and allow themselves to be happy in this life with the knowledge of the Plan of Salvation. The plan that the Lord prepared for us.

Time was flying during the mission. Elder Nichols and I were working hard and teaching a good number of people. We made a great effort to share the gospel of Jesus Christ anywhere and every time we had the chance. One day, we were at a convenience store, and I saw a candy that looked very good, but it was hard to tell if that candy had chocolate or coffee. I asked a woman who worked there if it had coffee.

She got the information pretty fast and told me that it had no coffee. That was great, I could eat then. The woman looked at me curious.

— Are you allergic to coffee? – She asked.

— No. I am a member of the Church of Jesus Christ of Latter-Day Saints, and we have a commandment of health. Because of that, I don't eat or drink coffee, I don't drink alcohol, I don't smoke, and some other things – I explained.

— That's amazing! It's so important to take care of our bodies – She said with a smile.

We talked a little about the church and I gave her a pamphlet about the Word of Wisdom with our contact and the church's address.

— That was some good OYM, Irineu – Elder Nichols complimented.

— Thank you.

After a few days, a young man from the branch asked to go proselyting with us. It was great, but it was very difficult to bring his bike to Fukuroi (since he lived in a different city), so we decided to walk all day. We walked to all of our appointments and stopped people on the street. It was very fun. At the end of the night, after we were home, I laid down on my futon and felt exhausted, much more than I usually felt at the end of the day.

— Why do I feel so tired? – I asked out loud.

— Probably because we didn't use our bikes today – Elder Nichols answered.

— Yeah – I had to agree.

— Doing dendou with our bikes is definitely better – He commented.

— Yes, for sure. But I think that if our area wasn't so big, we wouldn't need bikes – I pondered.

— True – Nichols agreed.

That day we wouldn't leave Fukuroi, so walking all day hadn't been a problem, but it was interesting to me to think about the beginning of my mission, back when I didn't know how to ride a bike and Elder Cleaver and I walked a lot. It made me realize that now I liked using a bike, and actually missed it. It also made me realize that it had probably been a little hard for Elder Cleaver since he was already used to using bikes.

As the weeks went by, for some reason, I started to think about my dog, Tobby. I had this feeling that he wouldn't be alive for my return. It was just a quiet feeling, almost like a certainty inside my chest. I also realized that my family didn't mention him anymore, nor I saw him walking around or lying on the sofa with my parents, as he used to do.

One P-day I decided to ask.

— Where's Tobby, by the way? – I asked.

My sister covered her face and turned off the camera. She was definitely crying, that was a bad signal.

My parents didn't want to give me more bad news but carefully told me that he had died. Tobby had had a heart attack and died very quickly, without suffering. I was very sad about this news. We bought Tobby when I was seven years old, so he had been the only dog I ever had.

That night I called Elder Gish to vent a little. Interestingly, it had become something of a habit to call after Gish after a bad day. But he always listened and helped a little. Elder Nichols was also very supportive.

Either way, I was very determined not to let any bad news interfere with my work as a missionary, so I moved on.

During that transfer, we had a particularly good Zone Conference in Shizuoka. I loved going to the Zone Conference there. We needed to take a train and go north. After we arrived at the train station, we needed to get a bus to arrive at the church. At the church, it was possible to see Mount Fuji and I just loved to see the city on the bus. Japan is a beautiful country.

At the Zone Conference Sister Judd shared something that she heard once:

— It doesn't matter where we are, it matters where we are looking at – She said.

That was very wise and it made me pounder. An important gospel principle is to "Endure Until the End", and it has everything to do with this advice that Sister Judd said. Where are my current goals going to take me? Are they taking me closer to Heavenly Father or Farther away from Him?

The Conference was about the Book of Mormon, so in the end, President Judd made a mission challenge, we should use a Book of Mormon in our native language and read it in 100 days (until 100 days). It was an inspired goal. Specially during this difficult time when

I learned about my brother's challenges and the death of my dog. Reading the Book of Mormon in my native language every day helped me to be closer to Heavenly Father.

It is hard to describe, but I felt the Lord strengthening me. It was a very real power that made me feel better and happier. In my interview with President Judd, we talked about happiness and Enduring to the End. President Judd mentioned that studying the Book of Mormon daily and having personal spiritual experiences with the Lord was the Key to remaining strong in our faith.

— I've learned that being happy is, most of the time, a choice. We need to choose to stay happy and seek happiness — He told me during the conversation — Serving others and being close to Heavenly Father also helps.

Yes, it was true. Being a missionary made me happy, and maybe, part of that was because I was focusing on other people rather than myself. That helps us to develop charity.

17

We Help a Family to Move

It was a very fun transfer with Elder Nichols, but he was transferred and would be companions with Elder Horton in Kanazawa. I took a train with Elder Nichols, and we parted ways in Hamamatsu, where I would stay with Elder Gish and Cruz. Elder Sherman, my new companion, would meet me at that train station.

An interesting coincidence is that Elder Sherman had just finished his training with Elder Orsi. So, once again I would be companions with someone who had been companions of him. We thought that coincidence was funny.

Elder Gish, Cruz, and I did OYM around the train station. Since Hamamatsu was a big city, the train station was huge and full of people. That made the train station a perfect place to talk and meet new people. After one or two hours, Elder Sherman arrived and we headed back to Fukuroi.

Elder Sherman was a great missionary, he became a good companion and a great friend. He was half Japanese ("Hafu" as the Japanese call it) and studied the language a lot. Many missionaries used to say that he really had the Gift of Tongs and, although I agree with this statement, he studied really hard whenever he could. His effort to master the language was really inspirational and definitely worked.

We got along really well and that made our work easier. The days were passing fast and we always had many goals to talk to more people, find more people to teach, and set baptism dates. It was around this transfer that I noticed how useful my habit of writing every night in the Journal was. Every once in a while, I would check my journal for specific information about our day, people that we had met, and people we had taught. Of course, we also registered everything on our tablets, where mission leaders and future missionaries could also see it, but my journal was a great tool for me as well.

One day we did a koukan in Hamamatsu, I had gone to Hamamatsu so many times that I knew many members, including the bishop, and knew where many places were. But it was fine, I liked the area. Talking to Elder Gish we mentioned our new and old goals and everything we had accomplished as missionaries compared to what we still wanted to achieve.

I mentioned to him that I used to be very shy and had a goal to overcome that. Elder Gish seemed surprised.

— I think you already accomplished that goal – He said.

— Really?

— Yes. You are not shy – He said with a smile.

I was very happy that he thought that, and maybe it was true. It wasn't hard for me to stop people on the street. Actually, it hadn't been an effort for a very long time on my mission, I had even forgotten it had been a difficulty at the beginning of my mission until I started speaking about that with Elder Gish. The Lord had really helped me to overcome that, and I was so grateful.

After we were coming back to Fukuroi, Elder Sherman and I were on our bikes. After crossing a big bridge (after the train station) there was a big slope for many meters. Going down that slope on our bikes was always fun, but the wind in Japan was very strong. Sometimes the wind was so strong (for no particular reason) that I've seen people fall on the street because of it. The wind would sometimes stop us on that slope, being stronger than gravity, it was very impressive.

That day, the wind was going in our direction, so we were going very fast on our bikes. Sherman was behind me, and I was somewhat lost in my thoughts (since it was so common for me to take that route). I'm not sure if Sherman lost control of his bike or if he was trying to make a joke, but he came really close to me, and I was not waiting for that, so I turned left.

Our bikes collided and we rolled with our bikes for a few meters. It was probably the worst fall I had with my bike during my mission (and I fell many times). When my head stopped spinning, I was lying on the floor next to Elder Sherman and our bikes were a little ahead.

I looked at myself to make sure I was ok.

— Sherman, are you OK? – I asked.

— Yes, I'm fine – He said getting up – Are you well?

— Yes – I answered and noticed that I didn't have my shoes. Both of us had lost our shoes during the fall.

That detail made both of us laugh. Suddenly a Japanese woman approached us looking very concerned.

— Are you hurt? I saw the fall, do you need me to call an ambulance?

— Thank you very much, but I think we are fine – I said with a big smile.

The fall probably looked pretty bad for her to ask us that. But miraculously, we didn't get hurt. Elder Sherman did cut his hand, but he didn't want to go to the hospital and it really wasn't that deep, so it healed well after a few days.

Eventually, Elder Sherman realized that his passport was expiring, so we called the mission office to find out what to do. They said we would need to go to Meitou in Nagoya to take care of that. Especially because the passports of missionaries don't stay with them, they are kept in the mission office, which I think is very wise, missionaries are transferred so often that it would be dangerous for them to lose some documents. But the Elders would search for more information to tell us when we would need to go there.

After a few days, a family asked for our help because they were moving. They lived in Iwata and would move to Kakegawa, but didn't have anyone to help them. Of course, Elder Sherman and I were ready to help. The next morning the husband of the family gave us a ride to their apartment in Iwata and we started working.

They lived on the fourth floor and there was no elevator, so we helped move the fridge, stove, and other heavy objects to the car. He drove us to Kakegawa and we helped them put everything on the second floor of their new house. After everything was finished we had lunch with them and came back to our apartment.

We both were exhausted and sat on the floor.

— We can't stop or sleep – Elder Sherman said out loud.

— Yes, I agree – I said seriously – But I think I need a few minutes to rest.

— Me too.

— I'm going to stay on the floor, this way I know I'm not going to fall asleep – I said to him.

— Great idea. I'll do the same – Elder Sherman agreed.

I laid my back on the floor and probably fell asleep for a few minutes just like Elder Sherman. Still, we got up, then changed our clothes, and started working again. Helping the members made us very tired, but I was so happy to help them. Helping other people is one of the things missionaries are supposed to do.

The day for transfer calls was coming and we started to talk about who would stay and who would be transferred.

— We can both stay – I suggested.

— Sure, but if one of us leaves, who do you think it will be?

— I'm here the longest, so maybe me – I thought.

— No, I think it would be me. We have Brazilians with dates for baptisms. They need you – Sherman said.

— That's sweet, thank you. But any Brazilian missionary can do what I do – I said with honesty.

— I disagree. I've met other Brazilian missionaries and you are very good at teaching and talking to people. People listen to you – He said with a straight face.

That was very nice of him to say.

— Thank you. That's very kind – I said.

But it turns out that we were together for one more transfer. I was happy that nothing would change. It had become too common for me to stay with a companion for only one transfer, so I was glad that I would stay longer with Elder Sherman. Hopefully, he also liked it.

Eventually, it was time to go to Meitou and fix the problem with Elder Sherman's passport. Once we arrived at the mission office, we did something of a koukan. Elder Sherman left with one of the Japanese missionaries of the office and I stayed with Elder Salzl.

He was the mission recorder, so he had a lot of work to do. I sat on the couch and started to read a Liahona. We didn't know how long they would take, so, at first, we thought they would be back at any moment. Eventually, I didn't want to read anymore and just observed the office around us. The clock of the office was pretty beautiful, something I had never noticed before.

— This clock is beautiful – I mentioned.

Elder Salzl laughed a lot.

— Sounds like you're very bored – He observed. Maybe he was right – Do you want to help me?

— Sure – I said and walked in his direction.

He needed to put many records of the mission on the computer and later we had to organize mail that needed to be sent that same day. It was actually fun to do all of that work, it was just so different from the work that I usually did as a missionary.

He got all the mail that we had organized and we walked outside to go to the mail. Elder Sherman had been gone for so long with the other missionary, that it was probably safe to leave. I got the bike that Elder Salzl's companion was using and noticed it was the same bike that I had been unable to ride at the beginning of my mission.

Suddenly I got excited about riding that bike, I would definitely be capable now, but it had been so impossible to me when I was at Inuyama that I wanted to see how the bike would "feel". I followed Salzl around the streets of Meitou and noticed that the blue bike I was riding was indeed harder than the one I had. I could ride it, but the tires were very thin and the whole bike was lighter, which made it harder to balance the weight on it.

Still, I felt very happy to be able to ride that bike with ease. It was like a testament to a chapter of my life that I had overcome on the mission. We had lunch in a Chinese restaurant (the same one where I had dinner with Elder Wood, Orsi, and Cavalcanti on Christmas Concert Day) and Elder Sherman came back later.

He solved the problem with the passport, so we were free to go back to Fukuroi. On the long train ride, I was able to read the Book of Mormon and almost finish it (The whole mission still had the goal of finishing the Book of Mormon under 100 days, which I accomplished that same week). It's amazing how reading the Book of Mormon always is a great experience, no matter how many times you've read it before. During this study, I realized how important it is to be "humble".

As a missionary I noticed that humility was a great attribute to develop, that was very clear during the mission since I needed the Lord's help to do anything, especially learning the language. But I noticed that it was an attribute very important to any member of the church. Just like pride is what defeated many members, if we are humble everything will be fine, we will be able to hear and accept advice from the Lord, from our leaders, and even other inspired people.

In Fukuroi I also had my second birthday on my mission. The first had been on the MTC and it felt like such a long time ago. I bought a birthday hat at Daiso and the Landin family, who didn't know it was my birthday, gave us a box full of chocolate muffins. I placed a candle on one of the muffins and celebrated. Sister Judd called me and wished me a happy birthday, the Zone Leaders also called later. It was very thoughtful of all of them.

Later, the next week, the Matsui family invited us to their house. They wanted to have dinner with us. We went there on June 7th and I was very surprised to see that it was a surprise (and a few days late) birthday party for me. I was very moved by their kindness; they were always so nice to us.

In one of our last koukans that transfer, I went to Hamamatsu and spent the day proselyting with Elder Coelho. It was a great day, but the weather was very hot once again and that meant all the spiders were back.

The Elder's apartment in Hamamatsu was very close to a big lake and that meant that every once in a while we would see some big unusual animals close to the apartment. That night, after Elder Coelho and I were back at the apartment, we noticed that there were many spiders on the stairs.

For some reason, Elder Coelho gave me the keys to the apartment, maybe he thought I would have no problems with the spiders, but he was very wrong about that. He used his flashlight to see all the spiders around us while we went up to the second floor. We reached the door, but that was a huge spider on the wall on our left side. The spider was scary, white, and as big as my hand. I got the key and aimed for the lock, but my hand was shaking a little bit.

— The spider Is looking at us! – Elder Coelho said right next to me.

— How do you know? – I asked.

— Look! – He said pointing to the spider with his flashlight.

I looked at the spider and noticed that one of the spider's eyes was glowing in our direction. It was a creepy vision for someone who is afraid of spiders, like me. Suddenly, the spider came running in our direction and we both screamed.

— Open, Irineu! Open! – Elder Coelho screamed.

— I'm trying! – I said and for a miracle, I was able to open the door.

We both jumped inside the apartment and closed the door as fast as we could. I loved Hamamatsu, but it had too many huge spiders.

At the end of the transfer, Elder Gish told us that Elder Sherman would be transferred and I would stay in Fukuroi and be companions with Elder Ilg. It was funny how all the members were surprised by that, everyone, even on Eikaiwa, assumed that I would be the one leaving since it was the end of my third transfer there.

I knew Elder Ilg already, he was from Porto Alegre, so we knew each other from before our missions, although we were from different stakes. It would be fun and interesting to be his companion. I was sad that Elder Sherman was going away, as well as Elder Gish, who was finishing his mission. But that is how things work on the mission.

18

An Apostle Visits My Mission

Elder Coelho also had lost his companion, so he needed someone to be with him and that person was Elder Cleaver, who was in the Shizuoka area, but after Elder Sherman left, I would stay with them until Elder Ilg arrived at Hamamatsu.

That's what we did. I said goodbye to Elder Sherman at the Hamamatsu train station and headed to the Takatsuka train station (also in Hamamatsu). I spent a few hours with Elder Cleaver and Coelho and it was very fun. Eventually, Elder Ilg arrived and we both went back to Fukuroi.

Something that was very nice is that that was Elder Ilg's final transfer and Fukuroi had also been his first area. That meant that he had a deep love for that area, all the members, and many people that he had taught before.

Zone Conference was in Meitou and President Judd shared some great news. He said that in August an Apostle would visit our mission. He didn't say who the member of the Quorum of Twelve Apostles would be but encouraged us to prepare ourselves spiritually for that meeting.

Elder Ilg and I kept working and trying to speak with everyone. Until, one day, we met a very polite man who started talking to us about the gospel.

— Have you ever thought about what is the purpose of life or where do we go after we die? — Elder Ilg asked.

— Yes. Every day — The man answered.

— Really? Everyday? — I asked. Having those questions is common, I believe, but ask yourself that every day is not so common.

— Yes, because of my work — He said.

— Where do you work? — We had to ask.

— In a funerary — He answered.

Yes, that explained it. We talked to him about the Plan of Salvation and set an appointment to visit him again. Unfortunately, he wasn't very interested and usually was not at home, maybe because of his work. Either way, I felt very happy to answer some of his questions that day.

The new district leader, now that Elder Gish had finished his mission, was Elder Sato, the same Elder Sato who stayed in our apartment back in Inuyama when we went to Fukutoku to meet President and Sister Judd for the first time. He was fluent in English by now and I was capable of speaking Japanese, so there were no problems communicating anymore. Since he was serving at Fujieda, that gave me the opportunity to visit my old area a few times when we did koukans.

One day, closer to the end of the transfer, Elder Ilg and I decided to go to a neighborhood not very far from Fukuroi, still neither of us had gone there before. I got on my bike and went in the right direction. Around me, there were huge rice fields as far as the eyes could see. Because of that, I knew that at night there wouldn't be any lights, but that was common and our bikes had lights strong enough to guide us.

We talked to many people in that neighborhood, but it started to rain. It was annoying to work in the rain but I was very used to it.

During my time with Elder Sherman, we used to get so wet, working in the rain, that it ruined one of my pairs of shoes.

After we talked to a family, I noticed that the rain was uncommonly strong. The wing was stronger than usual, and the water was falling like a river. That gave me a bad feeling.

— Irineu, I think the rain is getting dangerous – Elder Ilg talked while looking at the night sky – Do you think we should go back?

I looked at my watch and saw that it was 19:30 pm. I would hate to stop working that early, also I wasn't afraid of a little rain. The problem is that he seemed to be right about not being a regular rain.

— What do you think of working for half an hour and then going back? – I suggested.

— Seems great.

But only ten minutes later, after talking with one more person, the was a big lightning that lighted the whole sky. I felt that we should go back.

— I think you're right, we should go back – I said – Don't you think?

— Yes. Let's go – He said.

We got our bikes and started riding back to Fukuroi. The rain was hitting me with great strength and the only light on the road was the light of our bikes. The rain made seeing the road ahead much more difficult. Suddenly there was a great lighting on the sky that illuminated everything around us. It was like a big lightbulb in the sky for one or two seconds.

My heart was beating very fast on my chest.

— We're going to die, Irineu! – Ilg screamed behind me.

I laughed a little but was just as worried as he. We got home as fast as we could. We barely closed the door and sirens on the whole city started to go off, telling people to stay home. A very scary sound that I didn't hear very often.

— Wow, it's a very dangerous rain, apparently – I said out loud.

Ilg agreed. When it was around 10:30 pm, we were in our futons, and the speakers of town started speaking again, but I couldn't hear very well because of the rain.

— Do you understand what they are saying? – I asked.

— No. But it's probably just telling people to stay home again.

— You're right – I agreed.

The next day we saw that there was a new message on our phone. The city hall had sent a text message to everybody in Fukuroi that there was a tsunami alert in town and we should be vigilant. It's a good thing that the Lord protected us and blessed the city because we were sleeping and would not see the message, but that was probably what the speakers were saying. I had no idea how dangerous that storm had been.

The transfer came to an end, but it would be different this time. Elder Ilg was going home, having finished his mission, and my new companion would be Elder Cavalcanti. I was surprised with the news, and a little worried. I considered Elder Cavalcanti a great friend and knew him well since we were together in the MTC for a period of time that was longer than a whole transfer.

But being companions (especially on the mission field) was different, and I was nervous that we wouldn't get along very well. The good side is that I knew that Elder Cavalcanti was very obedient to the mission rules and worked hard to be a good missionary.

Elder Ilg needed to go to the Mission Office on Monday and I would need to stay with other missionaries, so I went to Hamamatsu and stayed with Elder Coelho and Spilling (an Australian missionary). It was a fun day, and I liked the experience of being part of a trio for a little while. On P-day (Monday), while I was writing my letter to President Judd, a man called, he was going to check our stove (that wasn't working well).

— I won't be in Fukuroi today, so the best day to visit us would be from Wednesday – I told him.

— Do you live alone in the apartment? – He asked.

— No, I live with a friend.

— Is your friend Japanese? – The man was curious.

— No, he is Brazilian like me.

— But does he speak Japanese well?

— I think he speaks as well as me – I guessed. I had never actually seen Elder Cavalcanti speaking Japanese during our mission, but was sure that he spoke well.

— So, he is fluent! – The man said.

— Thank you – I said with a smile, not expecting the compliment. We were having that conversation in Japanese.

I love the Japanese people, they are so nice and polite. That night, we used our bikes to go to a restaurant that served "Udon" in Hamamatsu. I was following Elder Coelho and Elder Spilling was behind me on his bike. We were on the road right next to the cars on the street. We went up a huge slope and, on the top, I saw that the way down was surprisingly steep.

It wasn't safe to go slow with fast cars (at least that was what Elder Cleaver taught me), so I just went forward maintaining control of my bike as it got speed. I felt a cold in my stomach, the same feeling that I had on a roller coaster. It was scary and exciting at the same time. I got as fast as a car for many meters, maybe even for a kilometer. Eventually, I stopped my bike on a sidewalk next to Elder Coelho.

— That was crazy – I mentioned.

— It was so exciting! – He knew exactly what I was talking about.

Then Elder Spilling arrives next to us.

— This was awesome! It was just like a roller coaster! – He said with a big smile.

It was fun, but we took a different route going back to the apartment, just to be safe. The next day was transfer day, and Elder Spiling left for his new area. Elder Coelho and I waited for our new companions. Elder Cavalcanti would arrive in the morning, but Elder Antunes would only arrive in the afternoon.

The day was incredibly hot. It was one of the hottest days of my entire mission. We went to the train station and I saw Elder Cavalcanti there. Unfortunately, he had some bad news. The night before he had damaged his back tire and it had a big hole on it, maybe more than one. Sadly, that meant that he couldn't use his bike.

— We need to find an "Asahi" to fix your bike – I said – Coelho, is there an Asahi close by?

— I think there is one close to us. Let me see – He said and grabbed his tablet.

He checked his map and saw that there was an Asahi a few kilometers away. I was close if you used a bike, but walking under a bright sun on one of the hottest days of the year was a very long distance.

Walking wasn't a problem, but the sun was so strong that we were all very wet with sweat after only a few minutes. We stopped at a convenience store for a few minutes. There, I bought a bottle of water and drank the whole thing in under a minute (something I used to do often in the summer days of Japan). We kept walking for a long time and stopped at another convenience store.

This time we were very close to our goal. I saw a big sign written "Asahi" and got very happy.

— We did it! – Elder Coelho said and ran in front of us with his bike.

I followed him and saw that the store was completely closed.

— No! – I said out loud.

— Oh no! – Cavalcanti said.

We all sat in front of the door, on the floor. There was a nice shade there that protected us from the sun. There was a piece of paper on the door explaining that the store would not open that Tuesday. Elder Coelho started looking at his map again.

A man approached us, probably thinking it was weird for the three of us to sit in front of the store.

— Excuse me, I should tell you that the Asahi will not be open today – He said.

— Yes. Thank you – I answered.

— Our friend has a punctured tire – Elder Coelho explained.

— Do you know a place for me to fix this bike? – Cavalcanti asked.

Unfortunately, he didn't know. The other Asahi was so far away that we decided not to go there. However, we found a different bike shop that seemed to be open, and it wasn't very far.

After walking for about an hour, we arrived at a small store that seemed to be old. We entered the place and saw only one person working. An old man that seemed to be very nice. Cavalcanti explained the problem to him and he said he could fix it.

— Do you think this is the best price we can get? – Elder Cavalcanti asked me.

— It's our only option – I answered. None of us was willing to walk around the city for over one hour trying to find a better place.

— Well he looks very experienced – Elder Cavalcanti analyzed the man.

— Yes, I think so too – Elder Coelho and I agreed.

The man fixed Elder Cavalcanti's bike really fast and we went back to the Hamamatsu apartment. Elder Coelho had made a very strong "mugi cha" which is a popular tea in Japan and gave it to us to drink. It was very cold, so it was great. After Elder Antunes arrived to be with Coelho, Cavalcanti and I went back to Fukuroi.

Gladly, I was wrong to be worried about Cavalcanti. We were not together for very long (I will explain this better later), but the time we had together was great.

The day the Apostle would visit us arrived. It was Elder Soares, from the Quorum of Twelve Apostles. Elder Cavalcanti and I did our best to follow President's Judd advice to spiritually prepare for the conference. All the missionaries from our mission would be present and we would take a picture with President and Sister Soares.

The conference would be held at Meitou, so Cavalcanti and I slept in an apartment there with many other missionaries. Elder Orsi was there and saw me writing in my journal.

— Irineu, do you still write every day? – He asked me.

— Every single day – I answered.

— Amazing! – Then he turned to a different Elder — He never misses a day.

The next day we went to the Meitou church building. Elder Cavalcanti and I bought a quick breakfast at a convenience store and headed for the church before any other missionary, but soon after many Elders and Sisters arrived. All the Elders and Sisters, to be precise. President Judd and other missionaries from the Mission office helped to arrange positions for everybody, so we could take a mission picture with Elder Soares, his wife, and other general authorities.

Elder Soares could arrive at any second, so President Judd asked me, and another missionary called Elder Pooley to be at the front of the church so we would see when they arrived. We stayed outside for a few minutes when we saw the cars arriving. We went back inside, and everybody got in position for the picture.

Every missionary shook hands with Elde Soares and we had the conference. It was a beautiful conference, Elder Soares talked about hope, and about how to be good missionaries in general. There was a moment when we could ask questions and he answered.

At the end of the conference, Elder Soares gave a blessing on the mission, and it was beautiful. I felt the Holy Ghost in a very strong way, and I was sure everybody was feeling as well. That moment I got a stronger testimony that Elder Soares is indeed an Apostle of the Lord Jesus Christ, he spoke with authority and we could feel the Spirit when he spoke.

After the final prayer, the Spirit was so strong in the room that no one spoke a word. As we were leaving, we whispered to say our farewells, since no one wanted to do anything to drive the good feeling away from us.

After many weeks, President Judd asked us to share in a group on "Line" (with the missionaries) the words of the blessing that Elder Soares gave. I had written the blessing as I remembered in my journal, so I sent what he said. President Judd highlighted how no one wrote the exact same words. We had all written the same blessing, but the words that we used were different, and some people wrote things that other people didn't.

That was a very educational experience that Presidente Judd used to illustrate how, when a story is true, we never tell the exact same way twice and how more than one person never tells the same experience with the same words. That is a testimony of how the accounts of the First Vision were true and how the books of the Bible also are true, even with different apostles writing the same experiences with small differences.

19

The Furnace of Affliction

On the next P-day, I shared with my family the great experience I had. Elder Cavalcanti and I went to buy groceries and suddenly our phone started ringing. I was worried and looked at Cavalcanti.

— President Judd is calling – I said.

— What do you think he wants? – Elder Cavalcanti was nervous, as was I.

— I don't know – And I was afraid of the possibilities. The last time the President called himself, was pretty bad – Do you want to answer?

— No!

— Fine – I said and answered the call.

— Hello Elder Irineu! – He said with his happy and excited usual tone.

President Judd explained that many adjustments had been necessary on the mission and I would need to leave for another area called "Tsu". It was in the prefecture beneath Nagoya, called "Mie", and it was the last Zone before the Japan Kobe Mission. I was shocked, but said that it was OK, and I would prepare to leave the next day.

That night I called many members of the branch and said goodbye to them. It was very sad, and they were all very surprised. It was my fifth transfer in Fukuroi, so the members already joked saying that

I was a member and one of them. Sister Koide, the wife of the branch president met me the next morning and gave me a beautiful gift, a small hymnbook with pictures of me and all of my companions there. It also had a message from her and her husband and they thanked me for my work and for playing piano at sacrament meeting.

I will not say the names of my next two companions. I honestly don't have many good things to say about them, and I think they were, themselves going through hard times in their personal lives. So, to respect their privacy, I will not name them.

The next day, I said bye to Elder Cavalcanti and took a train to the Nagoya train station. There, I met my new companion and went with him to Tsu. He told me that he was the district leader of Tsu and I thought that was a great sign, it probably meant he was a good missionary and an easy person to get along with.

Unfortunately, I was wrong.

The city of Tsu was very different from the others I had seen during my mission, it was right next to the ocean, so the city was a little different, we were always close to the sea and our apartment was on the ground floor, but I could see from the window the sea. It was beautiful. The city was full of bridges and rivers and I loved that. Early in the morning, I could see many people practicing canoeing. It was a happy vision.

Tsu was also a big city, and the members of the ward were great. They were kind and were always willing to help. There were also other missionaries there in Tsu, they were the Abe couple. They were married and started their mission in Nagoya right after President Judd arrived, so we all had around the same time on our mission. Elder and Sister Abe were a ray of light in those difficult times.

It was September, so Sister Abe was already organizing the agenda for the next Christmas Concert and told me that.

— Can I sing in the Choir? – I asked.

— Do you have experience singing in choirs? – She asked me.

— Yes. I always sang in my stake choir, in Brazil.

— Can you read sheet music?

— Yes, I play piano – I answered.

— Perfect! So, you can sing.

I was very happy with that. But my companion was very difficult. He had no sense of humor, at least not with me, and it made me realize how I had been blessed with happy companions so far. He also didn't like to follow rules regarding our use of tablets, and every time I told him something he didn't like, he would stop talking to me for the rest of the day.

Because of that, there was a lot of silence between us every day. With the free time I had at night since he always would be far from me, ignoring me, I started to study more the scriptures and old Liahonas in English. If anything, it helped me to learn more from older Prophets.

I wanted to have a better relationship with him and decided to try harder. My brother had told me once that if you wanted to love your companion on the mission, you should serve them. That seemed a great idea, so I decided to cook my dessert, the "pavê de sonho de valsa". The last time I had had time to cook this dessert was with Elder Bahr. It was a lot of work.

I made the dessert and he ate, but didn't say anything.

— So… did you like it? – I was curious since he hadn't said a word.

— Sure. It's good – And that's all he said.

I gave a slice to Elder and Sister Abe and they were much nicer about it. Sister Abe loved it and asked me for the recipe. I gladly gave her the recipe, even though it was harder to translate from Portuguese to English than I had imagined. I was with this companion for about 4 weeks, but it felt longer than the MTC.

One day I was particularly sad and stressed and our phone rang.

— Moshi Moshi – That was "hello" in Japanese.

— Irineu! – The other voice said.

— Orsi! – I was very happy to hear him – How did you get this number?

— It wasn't very hard – He said – I just felt like calling you.

We talked for a long time and I felt a lot better after that conversation. I was very grateful for his inspiration to call me. I don't think he suspected anything, but he was definitely following inspiration from the Lord and I was grateful to him and the Lord.

At the end of our transfer together, my companion and I took a bus to visit someone we were teaching with another member. Unfortunately, that bus didn't accept my "Monaca card" that I had used so far on my mission. The ticket was 300 yen and we paid the moment we left the bus.

I started counting my coins. My companion wouldn't help and I wasn't completely sure I had that amount of cash with me (even though 300 yen is very little) I had my "white mon", but I didn't want to pay 300 yen with a 10,000 bill, it would be too much. I started counting my 10-yen coins, I had so many I was pretty sure it would be fine. But I was tired and kept counting wrong over and over again.

Suddenly a hand placed two coins of 100 yen in my hand. I looked to my side and saw an old man with a very kind, smiling look in his eyes. He made a signal of secrecy as no one needed to know that and left the bus. I thanked him, but I never saw him again. The action of that kind stranger touched me very deeply. It is amazing how good people can be.

On another day we went to Meitou, for a Zone Conference. My companion was not speaking to me that day, but I was used to that. I sat on the second roll of chairs and my companion sat two chairs behind me. Some moments passed, I was reading Preach My Gospel and noticed that many people had arrived, including President Judd.

I looked to my right and there was my companion with a great smile and attitude. That made me very mad, although I didn't say anything at the moment. I understood that he didn't like me and made no effort to, but pretending to be best friends in front of President Judd was very annoying.

Transfer Calls finally came, and my companion was transferred. He loved Tsu in a very strange way. I think it was because we had wi-fi in our apartment, a terrible temptation to many missionaries. I talked with President Judd about the wi-fi and told him that I would unplug the wi-fi often, he approved that idea.

My companion would leave and was not happy about it, I was radiant but tried not to show too much. However, my next companion wasn't very easy as well. He was relatively new on the mission and for some strange reason hated to do missionary work. During that transfer, I also became a district leader and had many beautiful experiences with other missionaries, which helped me a lot.

My new companion also loved to complain about everything, but he had some problems dealing with depression. I have met many missionaries with depression and people who had to return home to take care of their health, so I could tell that my companion's problem wasn't very serious. It seemed he was just sad about being a missionary, but it isn't my place to judge and only the person who is going through adversities knows their own problems and difficulties.

I tried to help him and be nice. He was much nicer than my previous companion, so it wasn't so bad. The only problem was that he spent the whole day complaining about the way we did missionary work, where we went, how we taught, and many other things.

One day I decided to help him feel better. I would let him prepare our entire lesson without him realizing it.

— So, what do you think he needs to listen to right now? – I asked about the person we would teach that day.

He answered.

— What will be our goal? What will be our invitation for him to act? – I kept asking and writing down his answers.

After we finished, I said:

— We finished, perfect! What do you think of our lesson?

— I think it's bad – He said with an annoyed look.

— Why? – I was very surprised with his answer.

— I think we can do better. This lesson doesn't seem to be very inspired – He said with accusing eyes.

— You do realize you planned the entire lesson, right? – I had to say.

He was shocked and speechless for a few seconds. After that day I just accepted the fact that he was impossible to please.

We started to argue more as time passed by and I decided we needed to fix that. I waited for DKK and on the final part, where we should talk about our companionship, I said:

— I think we need to talk honestly with each other

— About what? – He asked.

— Well... we are not getting along very well, and we are arguing a lot. So, we should talk and solve our differences – I said.

— I think we are fine – He simply said.

— Really? – I asked.

— Yes.

— Can you list the reasons why we get along so well? – I asked.

After that, we had the worst argument we ever had. However, after everything was finished, and we told many truths to each other, we actually started to get along better. That made me think that honest conversation is always good, even if it isn't very friendly.

In October that was a great typhoon that damaged some areas on the Japan Nagoya Mission and other places in other missions, but in Tsu, there wasn't any great damage, gladly. We had to stay inside our apartment, of course, and I kept an eye on our phone. We were right next to the sea and surrounded by a river, so if the city hall sent a message telling us to leave, we had instructions to leave our apartment and go to the apartment of Elder and Sister Abe.

My companion used this time to sleep a little bit, but I was awake to keep an eye on the phone. Gladly, nothing bad happened and we didn't have to run to get out.

On one special Sunday, a member who usually helped us a lot said that he had invited a friend to eat lunch with the members after the meetings. I was very happy and said that was a great idea.

— Can you come with me? – He asked.

— Of course we can! – I said very happily. I was very excited to encourage members to engage in missionary work.

After the church meeting, we walked outside the church and I followed the members.

— So, where does your friend live? – I asked. If we were walking there, it would be close.

— I don't know – The member answered.

— Really?

— Yes. I met him today – He told me with a smile.

— I see.

Interesting. We kept walking and reached a group of people who were sitting on the floor. They were all drinking beer (and it was midday). The member came to one of them and said:

— Hello! Remember me?

— Yes! You are the man who invited me to have lunch right? – The man said. He looked drunk.

— Yes. Are you coming? – He asked with an engaging smile.

— Sure – The man said and got up.

I shook his hand and introduced myself and my companion. The more we talked, the more nervous I got. Usually, we like to introduce the church a little bit and explain how everything works. But this man had never heard about the church before, he wasn't even a friend of the member. The member only met him on the street and invited him to go have lunch at the church.

I loved that the member invited someone, but I started to get very nervous about how the man would behave at lunch with the other members. He was drunk and if he did something bad the members could get angry with us, and I would understand.

It was a short walk back to church and my chest was heavy with fear for the next few hours. However, once I entered the sacrament meeting room, I just felt peace entering my heart. It was completely sudden, almost literally as the Holy Ghost had cast away the bad feelings of my heart.

I realized I was not taking into account the sweet Spirit that exists within all church buildings. I was so used to the Spirit at church, that it was easy to forget about it. I was even judging the man a little bit. But everything went well during lunch and we had a great conversation with him, where we explained more about what we believe in.

A member of the Tsu branch who had just returned from her mission sat next to the man and talked with him for a long time. She was a great missionary. I learned many lessons that day.

My companion didn't care about any of that, he didn't even talk to the other man and didn't say a word about it after we left church. He wasn't worried about the man, but he also didn't really care about him at all.

While I was in Fukuroi I met a missionary that was already finishing his time as a missionary. His name was Elder Magalhães, he told me about a very hard time he faced and said:

— Every missionary has a Furnace of Affliction, but we can't give up – He said.

I liked how he spoke of not giving up. But at that time, it seemed a little dramatic to call a place a "furnace of affliction". But Tsu was definitely mine. That also made me realize that a belief that I had was correct, a place is never bad. There's no such thing as a "bad area", but some places will be better than others because of our attitude, our companions, or the other difficulties we might be facing.

Tsu was a beautiful place, easy to do missionary work, with great members, but the difficulties I had with my companions made my memories of the place a little dark.

20

After Much Tribulations Come The Blessings

Transfer Calls came again. I was excited and afraid about my next companion and my next transfer. That had been rumors that year about the time of the mission changing. Some people and rumors said that Elders would have missions as long as the Sisters (six months less). I often wondered how I felt about those rumors, I wasn't sure if I liked it.

However, the last few months had been so difficult for me that the idea of someone saying to me that my mission was over wasn't bad anymore. Still, I was determined to be a great missionary for whatever time I had left, and it seemed that all the rumors were wrong anyway, since nothing had changed.

The Zone Leaders told me everything that would change the next transfer for our areas. They also told me that next transfer I would remain as district leader and would train, but not alone. I would be a co-trainer and co-district leader with the first companion I had in Tsu.

To say I was stressed, sad, or desperate would be an understatement. The idea of being his companion again was terrible enough, but training someone would be much worse. I would normally love to train, but the beginning of the mission could be very difficult and normally was for everyone. So, having trainers who hated each other wouldn't help. Suddenly I was also worried for the new missionary too.

The next day I decided I needed to talk with someone, I was going crazy alone. I never told anyone about my problems with my former companion (neither with the current one), and I didn't like the idea of saying bad things about my companions of former companions to any missionary. But I needed to talk to someone.

Back in Fukuroi I would call Elder Gish, and sometimes I also called Elder Salzl to talk a little bit, after work, but it wasn't very often with Elder Salzl. Now, I was the district leader, so I supposed I could talk with the zone leaders. Elder Barton was a great missionary and I liked him a lot, so I called.

— Elder, I need to be completely honest with you, I'm freaking out – I said with honesty.

— What? Why? – He asked.

I explained how hard the last transfer had been to me.

— We're supposed to "love our companions" and for my entire mission I was able to do that, but with this Elder, I failed – I explained.

He tried his best to comfort me and say everything would be fine, but just saying all of my worries out loud made me feel better. On Monday, Elder Sato and my new (former) companion arrived at Tsu to stay with me. We had a meeting with President and Sister Judd where they gave us great pieces of advice about how to help our new companions.

It was great to see Elder Sato again and he would train as well. I had prayed a lot during those days and the Lord blessed me with faith that everything would be fine. I had no idea how things would work out, but I felt they would.

While I was walking with my companions (including Elder Sato) in the Meitou Church building, I saw Sister Galdino walking in my direction.

— Galdino shimai! It's so good to see you – We shook hands.

— It's great to see you too, Irineu! Are you going to train someone?

— Yes. Are you?

— No. I'm going home. I have finished my mission – She said with a smile.

I was very surprised.

— What?

— Yes. This transfer was my last – She laughed with my surprise – Time flies, right?

— It does – I agreed and said goodbye to her.

I walked with my companions to another room and felt a little sad. "I wish my mission was ending right now", I thought. The last months had been so hard, and the next two transfers apparently would be hard as well. At that moment, I felt that it would be better if the rumors had been true and my mission was ending at that transfer.

There, among all the missionaries who would train, I met another person, Elder Pangilinan. He was a Filipino missionary with whom I never had the chance to talk before. He was very nice and always very smiley.

The following day we would meet our new companions. While the President and other missionaries for the office were teaching them about the mission, the trainers went to the sacrament meeting and we started practicing the hymn "I Am A Child of God". We wanted to sing well and be singing when they entered, but we had no idea when they would, so we just kept singing for a long time.

Eventually, nine missionaries entered the room. I looked at them and tried to guess who would be our companion. I had a feeling that it would be a really tall Elder who was probably American. There were no Brazilians arriving for that transfer and that would probably be a problem for Elder Pangilinan, he had told me that he needed someone who could speak Portuguese because of some people he was teaching.

Apparently, I was wrong: the tall missionary, who was called Elder Davis, was Elder Pangilinan's new companion, and another missionary would be our companion. To be fair, my former companion seemed to be trying hard to make a good impression on the new Elder, I even got the impression he would try to do good work in Tsu. Our new companion seemed to be very nice as well.

One of them went to the bathroom, so I was in the hallway of the church, and that is when President Judd walked in my direction.

— Elder Irineu, I need to talk to you – He told me and I walked in his direction – I have not decided anything yet, but it is possible that you will need to be Elder Pangilinan and Davis's companion in Toyota.

I was completely speechless and tried to control my reaction at the same time.

— Now, I know that you love Tsu, but would you do this if it was necessary? – He asked kindly.

— Yes, I would. I trust you, President Judd, so whatever you decide I will do – I said honestly.

I didn't even know what to feel at that moment. I was definitely relieved, but I also had spent the last four days praying and accepting in my heart to be companions with that Elder again. I had decided that I would try my best to make things better this time, and as a trio, maybe things would indeed be better, the dynamic would certainly be different, but I had never been in a trio before. So, it was hard to tell.

— I haven't decided anything yet – President Judd said again – But do your best to explain everything in the area to your companions today. Don't tell anyone, please.

— I won't – I told him.

That was a big revelation, maybe for both of us. It was undoubtedly an answer to my prayers. It was amazing how the Lord was kind to me and always answered my prayers.

That night the three of us went to Tsu and to Elder and Sister Abe's house, they wanted to meet the new missionary. The next day

I kept my promise and explained the whole area to my companions. My former companion wanted to do it the next day, but I asked him to trust me on that. At first, he wasn't so happy, but later I think he noticed I wasn't telling him something.

That same night, President Judd called. He told me to pack my bags because, on the following day, I needed to go to Toyota in the morning. I explained everything to my companions and did my best not to look relieved. The new Elder seemed to be very nice, and I liked him, so I wished in my heart he had a great experience in his first area. Maybe he had. My former companion looked sad, which was very surprising for me, but the next morning he was very happy, so maybe he was relieved as well.

The next morning, I took a train to Nagoya Station. On the way there, I sat next to a family. I held my bike (inside the bike bag) on my right side and set next to a Japanese father with a child. On his left side was his wife.

The kid looked at me for a long time, then whispered something to his father.

— You can ask him – I heard the father answer.

— What is inside the bag? – The boy asked looking at my bike bag.

— My bike – I answered and opened the bag a little for him to see it.

He thought that was very cool. After that, I had a great conversation with the family. I told them I was a missionary and was moving to Toyota. They were also going to the Nagoya train station but would go to a different prefecture. I handed them a card from the church and said goodbye.

At the Nagoya train station, I met my new companions, Elder Pangilinan and Elder Davis. They were very nice and I followed them to Toyota. Elder Pangilinan tried to teach me how to pronounce his name correctly, but it was very hard, I thought I did it, but he always said:

— I'm sorry, it's not quite right. But you can just say Elder "Pang" – He suggested.

— Elder Pang is easier – I said with a smile. After that, Davis and I always called him Elder Pang, but every once in a while, I would try to pronounce his name right. I never succeeded, though.

For the rest of the transfer, Elder Pang and I trained Elder Davis and were district leaders. It was actually great, and I loved the experience. They were great missionaries. They were dedicated, hard-working, and very fun. On our first DKK together, when talking about our companionship, we decided to say something that we liked about each other, but it was too soon to say something we could improve with each other.

— You're both great Elders – I said – I'm just very grateful you both work hard, are obedient to the mission rules, and have a great sense of humor – I really missed people who could make a joke during the day.

Not sure if they noticed that I didn't have great relationships with my previous companions, but I didn't tell them.

— You're just so kind, Elder Irineu. I don't think I ever had a companion like you before – Elder Pang said.

After that, I had great transfers, some of the best of my entire mission. I am so grateful my mission didn't end that day when Sister Galdino left. I think about that sometimes, if my mission had ended at that moment, my final experiences would have been pretty sad, but I had great experiences and saw many miracles after that and ended my mission on a happy note.

You'll see.

21

Reaping Rice

The days went by very fast in Toyota. I had told my family that I would train in Tsu with my former companion, so they were very surprised when I told them that I was at Toyota with different companions. Elder Pang was from the Philippines, so we went to church in the morning, for me to talk with my family and around 16:30 for him to talk to his family. Elder Davis would choose a time that was better for him and his family, normally it would be the same time as me.

Davis was already very good at Japanese, but Elder Pang and I decided we would take turns helping him with language study in the beginning. Starting to study a new language can be very overwhelming and you might not know where to start, we all knew that. Elder Cleaver helped me a lot in the beginning with my Japanese study.

Like Elder Cleaver, Davis would tell me that I was very sassy and found that very fun. The training on the mission took 12 weeks to complete, but Elder Davis's training was different from my training. For some reason unknown to me, the mission was not using the "12 Weeks Program" when I had been trained, we used a different material. But, studying the program to help Elder Davis, I thought the 12 Week Program was amazing, and really taught useful things about life on the mission and how to teach other people.

Around that time I also read the "Adjusting to Missionary Life" book and wished I had read it before going out on a mission, or at least at the beginning of my mission. That book explains that losing appetite is common at the beginning of the mission and that was funny to me because in the first few weeks of my mission, I was never hungry (and lost weight because of that).

The city of Toyota was very beautiful. I don't think I ever thought a city in Japan was ugly, but Toyota seemed special for some reason. The city was very big and the streets were big and had many trees of many different colors. Not too far from our apartment, there was a big stadium that held many games for the city, and we could see the stadium from our apartment window. In order to reach the stadium there was also a big bridge that was definitely the most beautiful bridge I have seen in Japan, it was modern and had a space for cars and a big space for people to walk and ride bikes on the side.

We were also teaching many people in Toyota. In one of our first days together, we visited a couple of Brazilians. They were very nice people and very kind, but the wife had some strong beliefs that were different from what we learned in the gospel of Jesus Christ. The husband was very quiet and almost never spoke a word during our meetings, however, he was a good person and was reading the Book of Mormon every day. That showed us that, even though he almost refused to speak, he really was listening to us.

On the first night, we talked to them, we had a nice conversation where I introduced myself to them. Eventually, we started to talk about the restoration and how the prophet Joseph Smith restored the gospel of Jesus Christ and now we had a living prophet and apostles.

The wife told me that she had a problem with believing in a living prophet. That was new information, according to what Elder Pang had told me about them, so I listened mindfully to what she said. I explained to her that the Lord loves us as much as he loved the people in the Bible and gave us a prophet to guide us today the same way He did thousands of years ago. The Lord is the same yesterday, today, and forever.

Eventually, Elder Davis and Pang shared their testimonies with us and I translated what they said to the people we were teaching. Amazingly, their testimonies were exactly about what we were speaking. They spoke of their certainty that Joseph Smith was a prophet of God, the same way that we have a prophet today.

After I left the house I said:

— So, you two can understand a little of Portuguese?

— No – Elder Pang answered.

— Not at all – Elder Davis said.

— But your testimonies were exactly about what we were teaching – I told them surprised. I thought they had somewhat followed the lesson.

— What? That's amazing! I had no idea – Elder Davis said excitedly.

It really was. That is what happens when you are guided by the spirit, I think. We were also teaching another woman who had a firm testimony of the Book of Mormon and the church. In our first conversation, she told me about her belief that the Book of Mormon was the word of God, the same as the Bible, she also said that she wanted to be baptized.

— Well, if I can ask, what is keeping you from being baptized? – I asked.

— I work on Sundays. I was only able to go to church once, after that my shifts changed, and I worked every Sunday – She explained – It's sad because I loved the church.

— I see. Well, let's pray that something changes and you are able to go to church again – I suggested with a smile and she loved the idea.

She wasn't the only person we were teaching facing that problem. We were also teaching a man from the Philippines that worked on Sunday, so couldn't be baptized yet. He knew a little bit of English but was better at speaking Tagalog and his native language was a different language also from the Philippines called "Cebuano". Elder Pang could speak Tagalog with him and many times a member from the Toyota ward who also spoke Cebuano would go with us and speak a lot with him.

I and my companions prayed a lot that they would be able to go to church, and after some weeks, there was a change with the man's job and he was able to go to church after that, we were very happy.

One day Elder Davis said:

— It's so cool how we meet people from everywhere in the World. Like, the three of us are companions, and we have someone from Brazil, from the Philippines, from the U.S.A. – He mentioned – We are also teaching people from the Philippines, from Brazil, from India, from China, and from Japan.

— It is very cool! – I said.

It really was amazing. The world is full of different cultures and nations, but the gospel of Jesus Christ brings us all together. It doesn't matter where we are from or what language we speak, we are all a part of the Lord's Nation. That is truly a beautiful principle.

One day, we did a koukan with other missionaries. I stayed in Toyota with another Elder, and both of my companions went to a different area. While I was at Toyota I talked with the missionary and he explained to me that he was facing some challenges, he was having trouble getting along with his companions and started talking about different things that happened.

I started to think about what I should say and what should my advice be, but I had a feeling that I should just listen. That wasn't the moment for me to speak, it was the moment to listen honestly to the other Elder. So, I did that. The other missionary talked for a long time, and while he was talking (and I was paying attention to what he was saying) I cooked lunch, served and then we said a prayer to bless the food.

— Wow. You know what, Elder Irineu? I feel so much better! I just had all of that inside of me for some time – He said with a big smile – You are a very wise person.

I laughed a little bit.

— I didn't really give you any advice – I answered.

— I know, but I feel that you really know what the other person needs.

Later that day we talked a little more and I told him some things that I had done that helped me with my companions, especially when I had a hard time.

The next morning, we went to the train station and I noticed that I was happy to see Elder Davis and Pang again. I had missed them, and that was a feeling that I hadn't had about my companions for some time. Later that day, we were all riding our bikes around Toyota and we stopped to look at our maps. At that moment, a man stopped me.

— Elder Irineu! – He said happy. He was a member of the Hamamatsu ward called brother Miyazaki.

We talked with each other for some time and he left. It had been nice to see him again. My time in Fukuroi was great and I had great memories of Hamamatsu as well.

— Was he from one of your old areas? – Elder Davis asked.

— Actually, he is from Hamamatsu – I answered.

— I didn't know you had served in Hamamatsu – Elder Pang mentioned.

— I didn't. But I was in Shizuoka for a long time and went to Hamamatsu a lot – I explained.

For the first few weeks, I didn't have a table in our apartment, since there were only two tables in our apartment. So, I used the living room table. For that to work, we removed the sliding door between our "office room" and the living room, which made the whole apartment bigger and was a great change in all of our opinions. Eventually, a member from the ward gave us a table that she didn't use, and we placed my table between the other two.

On November 26th, 2019, we left early our apartment to help brother Suzuki. He was going to reap rice on a farm far away and asked for our help. We wore appropriate clothes (that we wouldn't mind getting really dirty) and went in his car to the farm.

I used a boot that he had and used a scythe to cut down big pieces of bamboo (that were really close) and built small towers with the bamboo. After that, we used the scythes to harvest the rice and tied everything to place on the towers. They would be ready to go home after some time. It was a fun experience, and we were happy to help.

We were all very tired after that but kept working for the rest of the day. Two days later was the day that President and Sister Judd had invited us to eat dinner with them, we would celebrate Thanksgiving together. Since it was only at night, we decided to have our DKK first and then go.

During our DKK, I looked at Elder Pang's desk and saw something that was always there, a small toy of a bird.

— Pang, why do you have an ostrich on your desk? Where does that come from? – I asked.

— Oh, it's not an ostrich, it's an emu, and that's a funny story. But to summon up, an Australian sister gave me that because she knew I loved the "Great Emu War" – He answered with a smile.

— Then, what? – I asked already thinking the name was funny.

— The "Great Emu War" – He repeated and looked to Edler Davis – Don't you know that war?

— No – We both replied.

— Ok. So, many years ago, in Australia, the number of Emus in the country was too big and it was starting to become a problem. So, the government gave authorization for the army to attack the emus and kill many of them. They basically declared war on the animals – He explained.

— And what happened? – I asked.

— When they shot the animals, the Emus attacked them. They even hurt or killed some soldiers – Elder Pang answered.

At that point, I started laughing. It was such a great story but seemed to be a lie of how absurd it was. I believed Elder Pang the story was true, but that only made me laugh harder. Eventually, both of them also started laughing, since I just couldn't stop.

And that is how our DKK was ruined. Every time I looked at that toy, I would start laughing again and they would soon follow. Elder Pang hid his toy, but at some point, we gave up our DKK and headed to Meitou. I would still laugh on the train to Meitou, and even during dinner, but I was better able to control myself then.

In order to get to Meitou, we used a different train line that was very beautiful and modern. The train was magnetic and I barely felt it moving. It also had a great view. We got to President and Sister's Judd house and saw many other missionaries who had also been invited. All of them were close to the mission office's area, like us.

I looked around the house and saw a beautiful clock. It was made of wood and it was my size, or even higher. President Judd noticed me admiring the clock.

— Did you like the clock, Elder Irineu? – He asked.

— Yes, it's very beautiful.

— Let me show you something.

He opened the clock and showed a tiny inscription in a golden square. The inscription had a name: "Gary E. Stevenson".

— Is this Elder Stevenson? – I asked impressed.

— Yes, he was mission president of Nagoya some time ago – President Judd explained.

I knew Elder Stevenson had served his mission in Japan and was mission president of another mission, but wasn't sure it was Nagoya. That was nice information. There, in the mission office, I saw Elder Cavalcanti and others that I knew, like Elder Soneja, who went to Fujieda after I left, but now was in a different area.

While I was there, Elder Bahr called me, he was one of my zone leaders:

— Where are you? – He suddenly asked – I can hear President Judd.

— Yes. We are at the Thanksgiving at his house.

— That's nice, but it isn't your first Thanksgiving.

— True, my first one was you and Elder Buchanan. I mean, that counted, right? – I wasn't sure, so I had to ask.

— Of course it did! – He said almost offended.

— Great – I said.

But this Thanksgiving was very special. Sister Judd cooked a great dinner and after eating, President Judd explained a little about the holiday and we all said things we were grateful for. Everything was over around 21:15, and Elder Pang and I started being worried about going home, we would probably be late. However, President Judd explained that we would sleep at the mission office, the bedroom was huge, and everyone would fit. That solved the problem of the time.

11 elders slept in that apartment. It was fun.

22

Did You Hear the Angels?

We couldn't waste any time, so the next day we woke up very early and left the mission office at 5:30 am. I, Elder Davis, and Pang got ready for the day in absolute silence because all of the other Elders were sleeping. We left the building and walked on the silent and empty streets of Meitou. The sky had some light, but the sun was not yet visible.

The air was very cold and the wind was pleasant. I always thought that kind of cold wind and temperature was very invigorating, and always made me smile. It was 3°C (37.4°F).

— It's so good! – I said with a big smile when the wind hit my face.

At the exact same time, Elder Davis said:

— It's so cold! – He looked at me with the corner of his eye – Shut up!

We arrived at Toyota around 7:40. We got ready, I took a shower and we left toward Seto, to have a District Council Meeting (DCM) there. After DCM, I and Elder Davis stayed with Elder Bahr for a koukan in Toyota. It was fun to do missionary work with Elder Bahr again.

The days passed and the Brazilian woman we were teaching told us that she would go to Brazil and stay there for at least 6 months. I talked to her and said that in Brazil she could go to church on Sunday and even be baptized there since she was always working on Sunday in Japan. She loved the idea and said she was nervous about finding the missionaries. We convinced her to go find the missionaries and said we would send her information to Brazil, this way the missionaries would find her, and everything would be easier. She thanked us a lot.

I never heard of her again, but we did send her information to the missionaries in Brazil, so I firmly believe she got baptized in the church. Around this time a miracle happened with the man from the Philippines we were teaching. His shift changed and he called us very excited and said he would go to church next Sunday. We were all very happy and I said a prayer thanking the Lord.

It was December and the Christmas Concert Day was getting closer. Sister Abe put me in charge of organizing the Brazilian missionaries who would sing a song in Portuguese and send her pieces of advice and requests to them. We would sing "The First Noel" (which in Portuguese is called "Quando o Anjo Proclamou") and the main choir would sing "Wondrous Gift", "Oh Come, Oh Ye Faithful", and finally, ending the Concert, "Joy to the World".

On December 4th, 2019, I, Elder Pang, and Davis took a train and went to Meitou once again to practice all the hymns. Sister Abe had a lot of work putting everything together and we could all see how she was putting a lot of effort and faith that the Concert would touch the hearts of everyone there.

— I know that if we sing with faith, people in here will hear the angels singing about our Lord – She told us while we were practicing.

At the Christmas Concert, I saw many members from Inuyama. It was so good to see all of them again. I even saw someone who used to go to our Eikaiwa class (and we talked about the gospel with him many times) and he told me that he was baptized where he lived (in a different area). I saw members who had gotten married, and everyone seemed to be full of happy news.

I also saw Elder Sherman again. He was very talented at playing drums and would help a lot with the concert, with more the one presentation. He was training Elder Alison and they, with Elder Correa and Farias, would sleep in our apartment that night to go with us to the Christmas Concert. Elder Orsi and Cavalcanti were also going to sing at the Choir. This time, I didn't let anyone keep their tablets in my bag.

The Concert was beautiful. Every presentation was very well performed and all of the choir hymns had beautiful arrangements, especially Joy to the World. This last hymn we sang at the end of the Concert and I could feel the Spirit and a huge happiness that just wasn't common. The Spirit was definitely filling all of our hearts with joy.

After we had finished, I walked down the stand and Sister Endou, from Inuyama, came to me.

— Elder Irineu, Congratulations! Everything was so beautiful, this last hymn made me feel so much happiness that I felt it just there wasn't room in my heart for it – She said with a great smile.

— Thank you! I also felt so good! – I told her.

I went to Sister Abe to congratulate her.

— Elder Irineu! – She said when she saw me – Did you hear the angels?

I felt it was a profound question, and it was also the answer to what we were all feeling. We all had felt the Spirit very strongly, so maybe angels really were present there, singing with us. It would be a wonderful explanation. And maybe, that was an answer and even a reward to Sister Abe's prayers and effort.

— Everything was so beautiful Sister Abe, congratulations! – I told her.

We all went to our homes and had a great night of sleep, after that wonderful night. The days passed and eventually, Transfer Calls Day arrived. President Judd told us that I would stay with Elder Davis, finish his training, and remain the district leader. Elder Pang, however, would be transferred to Okazaki and become zone leader.

We were all sad that Elder Pang wouldn't stay with us and finish Elder Davis's training. But two people training at the same time wasn't common at all, so it also wasn't a great shock that it didn't last.

On December 14th, there was a Christmas party in the Toyota ward. The three of us sang Silent Night and almost everyone we were teaching went to the church that night. We even met and invited a Chinese man who had loved the church, even though he didn't know much about Christianity. He soon told us that he wanted to be baptized, but we explained that we needed to show him the covenants and commandments that he needed to know before getting baptized. We also explained that he would need to go to church a few times before being baptized, but we were all very happy and excited about teaching him.

The day of the new transfer arrived and we said goodbye to Elder Pang. A few days later we needed to go to Meitou for something called "Trainers Report" where we would meet the other missionaries that arrived with Elder Davis and their trainers. There was, however, a problem.

The train station that we used to go back to Toyota after the Christmas Concert was closed and had no workers there when we arrived, because of that, I was not able to pay for my final trip to get to Toyota. In the following days, I went to that train station many times to pay for that trip, but there was never anyone working there. That day when we were supposed to travel to Nagoya, it was no different, I had no luck. There wasn't anyone there for me to pay for the trip and, because of that, my card was blocked since technically I had never finished my travel to Toyota (that caused an error on the card).

I would fix that problem later (I had been trying to fix it for many days), but that day I needed to get to the Meitou train station. So, Elder Davis and I went to another train station called "Umetsubo", from a different line, and took a train there. It would be a different route to Nagoya, one that I had never used, but it was the only way.

I was really worried about being very late since President Judd asked us to be there on time, so I said a silent prayer and looked on my phone at the best possible route. We would have to change trains at different stations at least three times, and that was a little complicated.

On the second train we took, I found the instructions very complicated, so it was better to ask someone. I turned to the woman next to me and explained where I wanted to get and asked if she knew the correct train for me to get next.

The woman was surprisingly nice and was ready to help. She also thought the instructions on the phone were too vague and asked me to wait for a second. I was unsure about what she was going to do, but waited with Elder Davis, who was even more lost than me. The woman had a husband who didn't look very happy about all the troubles they were facing to help us, even though the woman only took five minutes, so, I apologized for the inconvenience and the woman said it was no problem at all.

She walked with us to the second floor (on the underground) and told us to wait there for the next train. I thanked her many times and she quickly went away. Japanese people usually feel uncomfortable when you are thanking them. They are very nice.

After that, it was very easy to get to Meitou, and we arrived only two minutes after we were supposed to. I saw that as a great blessing since there were missionaries that arrived after us. That night I got a different card so that we could get to Toyota on time, and sometime later I fixed the problem with the other card.

That was not the only time when a kind person helped us in a moment of need.

Many days later, we were going to teach a Brazilian family one night. We had a lesson with a Japanese member and left his house to go to the Brazilians' house. The Japanese member already lived far from where we lived, but the Brazilian family lived much farther. However, that wasn't a problem with our bikes.

The only problem is that after we left the member's house, Elder Davis's front tire lost all air. We examined his bike and noticed that he probably had run over something very sharp that caused a hole. Either way, it was night so no Asahi would be opened and even if there was, it was way too far for us to get there by foot.

— Oh no – I said, already thinking about what we had to do.

— What are we going to do? – Elder Davis asked.

— We need to head back home if we want to get there on time. We can call the family and explain the problem – I answered.

And that was what we did. I called the family and told them that we would have to reschedule for the day after tomorrow. They were very nice about it and asked if we needed any help (they thought that it was reckless of us to take such long journeys on our bikes, but it really wasn't). Elder Davis and I started walking home.

— You don't seem angry – He mentioned.

— I'm not angry. It wasn't anyone's fault. These things happen – I said with honesty.

We actually had a great walk and talked a lot with each other. Davis was a very fun person and we had many of the same interests. We arrived just in time at our apartment, right before 21:00.

The next day, we had to fix his bike, so I looked on the map about how to get to the town's Asahi. I knew how to get there by bike, but that route would take much longer walking, so we would have to take a shortcut walking inside the town, instead of around it.

It seemed easier on the map. In real life, we got lost many times. We took that opportunity to talk with many people about the church. But eventually, we decided we needed to ask for information, even though there was nobody on that street.

We kept walking for some time and we stopped a nice old lady to ask her if she knew the right way to Asahi (which street we should take).

— I'm actually going to a hospital really close to that place. Let's walk together! – She said with a great smile.

She was a very nice person and the three of us had a great conversation. Eventually, she asked what we were doing in Japan and we told her about the church. We gave her the church's card, which had our number, and asked her to call us if she ever needed anything. With her help, we were able to get to the Asahi and fix Elder Davi's tire.

On December 24th, we visited a family of Brazilians from Toyota ward, and at night, we went to the house of the Mishima family, it was a great night, and in the end, we ate a Christmas cake, it was very nice. After we left their house, we took our bikes and ran to the apartment of the Chinese people we were teaching. We wished him a Merry Christmas and had a lesson about the Word of Wisdom.

The following day, it was Christmas and we went to Meitou to celebrate Christmas together. After lunch, we went back to our area and did some proselyting until the night, when we had Eikaiwa and taught a great lesson where we talked about Christmas and our families.

Christmas and New Year were great during the mission once more.

23

It Wasn't a Waste of Time

Elder Davis and I were very busy for the rest of the transfer. We were teaching three different people who were progressing really fast and I had hope that they would be baptized soon. All three people were from different nationalities, we were teaching a woman from India, a man who had recently arrived in Japan from China (we talked to him in English), and the same man from the Philippines we taught together with Elder Pang.

The Chinese man was excited to be baptized soon and showed great faith overcoming difficulties and receiving testimonies from the Lord about doctrines such as The Word of Wisdom and Law of Chastity. He prayed and felt those commandments were real and came from God.

However, one day we taught him about tithing, and he looked disturbed. He told us that the only reason he had moved to Japan was to make more money and that commandment was something that he could not accept. We talked more with him and I did my best to follow the Spirit. I explained to him that tithing was used to pay for the chapels, the materials we used at church, to build temples, and to help those in need. No one serving in the church received money from tithing. I also read many scriptures from the Bible that spoke about tithing, but his face was hard to read.

— If this is a hard doctrine and commandment for you to accept, it's fine. You need to pray and ask the Lord if this is His commandment – I explained – Not all commandments are pleasant for us at first. But paying tithing is not something you need to do for now. Actually, only members can donate tithing. So, you should take your time to seek the Lord and receive a testimony about tithing.

He accepted, but Elder Davis and I were very worried about him. The next day, a Sunday, we visited him again. This time, his mind was made. He told us that he didn't want to go to church anymore and, therefore, shouldn't have lessons with us. He said that he loved money more than he loved the Lord.

— I'm sorry that both of you wasted your time with me – He said with honesty.

Elder Davis quickly answered:

— No, it wasn't a waste of time – He said calmly, but very seriously – Our duty, as missionaries, is to bring people closer to Christ, and during our time together I feel that you came closer to him. So, our time with you was not wasted!

He spoke with authority, and it was impossible not to feel the Spirit in that room. I was impressed with Elder Davis, the way he spoke was how I imagine how people speak in the scriptures when it is said that they spoke with "power and authority". Our Chinese friend couldn't deny the Spirit he was feeling.

— I'm sorry, it wasn't a waste of time. You're right – He said with a new attitude.

— Can you do me a favor? – I asked – Even if you don't want to meet with us anymore, please keep reading the Book of Mormon. This book is sacred scripture and will help you to feel the Spirit of the Lord, as well as His guidance.

— I'll do that – He told me – I will keep reading it.

— Thank you. I know it will bless your life – I said.

I meant that. At that moment, he was not ready to accept the gospel, but I believe that one day in the future, he might. Sometimes people need some time, I saw it happen many times during my mission, I saw many people decide to embrace the gospel, be baptized, and be full of faith many years after meeting the missionaries. We should never lose faith in anyone.

With our Filipino friend, things were a little different. He knew that the church was true, and he had a strong testimony of the Book of Mormon and living prophets. However, he was a little afraid of his family. They were from a different religion, and he worried about what they would think about him being baptized in a different religion. Because of that, he was reluctant to be baptized.

There was a member of the church that frequently went with us to visit him. This member also spoke Cebuano, so he helped with communication and with his friendship. One day we were talking about baptism, and he opened up a little more about the subject:

— All I want is to come closer to the Lord and be clean of my sins – He said.

— Brother, without baptism you cannot be clean of your sins – I explained.

He was speechless and looked me deep in the eyes. I was being completely honest. Without baptism, we cannot be clean and enter the Celestial Kingdom. He was touched by our words and decided to be baptized.

It was a happy day when he accepted. His journey had been full of miracles, at first he couldn't go to church, but one day, his shift changed forever and he was free on Sundays. His family was also very kind to him and the Church of Jesus Christ of Latter-Day Saints, and eventually told him that he could be baptized, it wasn't a problem to them.

Now, he needed to be interviewed by the Zone Leaders. Normally, it would be a district leader, but since I was the district leader, it couldn't be me. Elder Pang came with his companion and Elder Pang's companion started the interview with our friend.

We were a little worried. As a district leader, I had the opportunity to interview many people and most of them were ready for baptism, but sometimes, people needed more time to fully understand the commandments from God that they would be accepting. Many times, people don't say their doubts to the missionaries, for some reason, and that is one of the reasons why the interview is very helpful.

Unfortunately, our friend was not able to be baptized at that moment, and we were all sad (including Elder Pang, who wasn't the one who made the interview), but he still needed time to follow one of the commandments correctly.

Many months after I finished my mission, the members from the Toyota ward called me and I was able to watch his baptism meeting. It was a very happy day for him, and for me (and for Elder Davis and Pang, who also watched the ordinance).

Our third friend, from India, was a very kind woman. She was incredibly kind and had a lot of faith. Before meeting the missionaries, she believed and many Gods, not just One. So, she had the belief that she needed to go specifically to the right shrine to pray to a specific God. With the missionaries she learned that God is our Heavenly Father, He knows and loves us, and we can pray to Him anywhere and anytime. He will always listen.

However, she still had one habit. At the beginning of her prayer, she would announce herself and say her name.

— Sister, Heavenly Father knows who you are, He loves you very much and when you pray, he knows it's you who are speaking – I testified to her, afraid that that important principle was not clear to her.

— I know, but He has so many children and so many other important things and problems to look after – She explained.

That conversation made me feel very humble. How grateful I am that Heavenly Father knows me. He is omniscient and knows everything about me, He knows me better than I know myself and knows what I need before I even ask. That is a deep and beautiful truth that I learned to appreciate more after meeting her.

She also wanted to be baptized and traveled to India to visit her family and tell them about her decision. Her plan was to be baptized after coming back. However, she told us that her family had forbidden her to be baptized. She explained that a cousin of hers told her parents that if she got baptized at the Church (a Christian church) she would fall into a lower caste in society.

Her parents were afraid for her after that and told her she couldn't be baptized.

— Is that true? – I asked very curiously – Would it be bad for your caste?

— No. I am pretty sure it wouldn't – She answered.

But we kept teaching her and praying for her. One day she told us that her parents were starting to like the Church and every Sunday, they asked her what she had learned in Church. This way she would share gospel principles with them.

Our transfer was coming to an end. Elder Davis and I talked about who would be transferred next, it could be any of us since we had the same time in that area. Actually, Elder Davis had arrived at Toyota one or two days before me.

In my interview with President Judd, he had exciting news for me:

— Elder Irineu, I usually don't say what's going to happen in the following transfer, but I will tell you that you will be training again – He said with a great smile.

— Really? – I was surprised.

— Yes. You did a great job and I want you to do it again – He said with confidence.

— Thank you, I will do my best!

I was very happy that he thought I did a great job and he trusted me to train one more time. This meant that my next companion would be my last. I was on my 14th transfer, and missionaries who were not Japanese only had 16 transfers on the mission.

So, on the following transfer calls it wasn't a surprise that Elder Davis would be transferred and I would stay in Toyota. But I was fine with that, I loved Toyota and the church members there very much. Elder Davis would be transferred to Toyohashi and be companions with Elder Sherman.

That was happy and surprising news to us all. During that transfer I had a koukan with Elder Sherman and so did Elder Davis, so they knew each other and were friends. At first, Elder Sherman thought I was joking when I said he would be companions with Elder Davis, but eventually, he believed.

On Tuesday, I would have to go to Meitou to receive training from President and Sister Judd about training other missionaries. After training, I went back to Toyota with Elder Alison and Elder Correa, who would stay with me until we all received our new companions.

On the next day, we received news that something had gone wrong with the travel from the missionaries, and for some reason that meant they would only arrive the next day. That meant I would do missionary work with Elder Alison and Correa for a full day, but they didn't have their bikes, so we would have to walk.

At some point in the morning, it started to rain, but it was a very faint and weird rain. The sky had a bright sun with only one cloud that apparently was the one raining above us. But the water felt different. I raised my hand and saw that it was tiny pieces of ice.

— It isn't rain or snow – Elder Alison said just realizing that the rain was different.

— It's hail, I think – I said. It was very cool, the first time I saw hail in Japan (but not in my life, there is hail in South of Brazil).

Gladly the hail soon stopped and we didn't get wet (or hurt). The next day we went to Meitou and got ready to meet our companions. I had just been through that process with Elder Davis, but was still a little nervous. We started to sing a hymn, but President Judd suggested that each of us sang in our native languages, since all the trainers and trainees were from many different nationalities.

We started to sing, but it was horrible, I could see on Elder McBride's face, looking at us, that it was horrible. Elder Wada was able to hide his emotions better.

— You all sound like... like angels – Elder McBride struggled to find the right word.

— But maybe we can organize better – Elder Wada suggested.

We all sang next to the person who also sang in the same language, which was next to a Brazilian sister, in my case. And the hymn sounded much better.

My new companion was a Brazilian called Elder Melo. He was almost as tall as Elder Davis and had red hair. He was a very nice person and I immediately noticed we would get along well. We arrived at the apartment and explained the whole area to him, then we left to speak with other people and preach the gospel. President Judd asked us to take the new missionaries to do some OYM the same night they arrived, and I was determined to follow that instruction, even though it was 0°C (32°F).

Elder Melo's baggage hadn't arrived yet, so he hadn't any big coats. I gave him my warmest one and used another that I had. We talked with other people for around one hour on the cold roads of Toyota and went back home. Elder Melo seemed to have liked it.

I was excited for the next and last two transfers. But I had no idea what was in store for me.

24

COVID Strikes

Working with Elder Melo was easy. He was always ready to help, he already knew how to ride a bike, and he wanted to work hard and be a good missionary. While doing his training, I noticed that his first 12 weeks had the inverse role for me of counting down my weeks in Japan. However, I was determined not to let that affect my work and had even talked about that with President Judd in my last interview.

One day, Elder Melo and I were visiting brother Suzuki. There were two brothers Suzuki in Toyota, one of them was Japanese and had lived his entire life in Japan, and the other was Brazilian and lived there for a few years. Both were wonderful people and helped us a lot. The Suzuki we were visiting was the Brazilian one. He told us about this new disease that had appeared in China and that was making people nervous around the world, he said the name of the disease was "COVID-19".

— Don't worry brother, I'm sure this disease won't be a problem for us, in another country – I told him with a smile.

I was completely wrong.

On February 15th, 2020, we received a new rule for our mission. As COVID was spreading and people didn't know much about this disease yet, we should never shake hands or hug anyone. Not shaking wands would be hard for me, since I did that with almost anyone I met on the street. However, in the Japanese culture, shaking hands is not that normal, so I would only have to fight my own habits, not the culture of that place.

But we kept working hard. One day, Elder Melo and I had a lesson with a Brazilian family in a neighborhood far from where we lived. So, we decided to knock on some doors. At first, everything went well, we talked with a family that had been living in Japan for a long time and we gave a Spanish Book of Mormon for the mother and a Japanese one for the son.

Right after that, Elder Melo went ahead to knock on a door. I looked at the door, right next to where people write their names (it is very common in Japan for families to write the names of the family living there in front of the house or apartment) and saw that in that house they belonged to a religion where the members were usually not very nice.

— Elder, no! – I tried to stop him.

It was too late, he knocked on the door and a woman quickly opened the door. Maybe he was right to knock on that door, everyone needs to have the opportunity to accept the gospel of Jesus Christ, but that woman was quickly very rude. She said that she, and her religion, didn't accept the "Mormon church" and many other denominations, such as "Catholics, and protestants", and that our church was false, as was the Book of Mormon.

— I respect your personal opinions – I said with a smile – But the correct name of our church is "The Church of Jesus Christ of Latter-Day Saints", and I can give you my testimony that the Church really is the church of Jesus Christ, that He restored on these last days. And the Book of Mormon is the word of God.

Real testimonies are important because people cannot argue with what you know to be true. But the woman quickly looked enraged, she had hatred in her eyes and said:

— No! It isn't! I bet the life of all of my children that it isn't!

At that moment I realized it was pointless to keep talking to her. She had not the Spirit with her, her heart was closed and nothing good would come from that conversation.

— Listen, lady, you speak with no charity, and I don't want to keep talking to you – I said seriously – Have a nice night.

I turned my back and left. She kept screaming with even more anger, but I didn't pay attention to what she said. My companion followed me, and we kept talking to people. Two other people were also rude, though no one was as aggressive as that woman.

Right before we knocked on the house that we would teach I suggested we said a small prayer, to bring the Spirit back. We prayed and I felt a great and peaceful feeling. The lesson was great, and the family agreed to go to church that week on Sunday, after that they would go to church every week.

That night, Elder Melo came to talk to me:

— Irineu, were you always like this? – He asked calmly.

— Like what?

— This... bold.

— You think I'm bold? – I asked really surprised.

— You tell people in their faces that they have no charity and walks away – He said as if it was obvious.

I laughed a lot.

— At the beginning of my mission, I made many goals of being more bold and less shy – I told him.

— Really? – This time, he was surprised.

— Yes, it was really difficult for me to stop people on the street. But now, it's one of the things I like the most about being a missionary.

The next day we visited a member of the church who had stopped going to church for many months. I'm not sure what had happened to him, but he had no faith anymore and, though more polite, had similar feelings to the woman we had talked to, the previous night.

— The history of Jesus Christ is 2000 years old, it didn't start in 1830 – He said. It felt like something he had heard and was repeating now.

— Well, the Book of Mormon was written 600 years before Christ – I said.

— No, it wasn't – He said.

— Yes, it was – I told him seriously.

— No, it wasn't – He repeated.

— Yes, it was – I said again. I was completely willing to do that all night.

Elder Melo decided to jump in and explained that the Book of Mormon was written by many prophets over centuries and that Joseph Smith had translated it by the power and gift of God. Then, I said:

— Brother, we are not here to argue with you nor even to prove anything to you, but I want to say that, during my life, I learned so much about Jesus Christ and God by reading the Book of Mormon – I said with honesty.

He seemed to be touched and changed his attitude. He said (more friendly) that he had read many things on the internet that had killed his testimony and crushed his faith in the Church.

— Have you prayed to know if the church is true? – I asked.

He didn't answer, and it seemed that he couldn't look me in the eye, at that moment. Eventually, we left his house and I felt very sad for him. People are free to make choices and believe in what they want. But, when in doubt, we should always pray. The Lord will never lie to us, and He will always help us to find the truth. I have a personal testimony that the Book of Mormon is true because I prayed with faith and received a testimony. And everybody that I ever met who prayed with faith, received the same testimony. Unfortunately, some people are not willing to pray

The next Sunday, many people that we were teaching went to church. However, the cases of coronavirus were spreading fast throughout Asia and the presidency of the area had determined that the Church would only have one hour (sacrament meeting), this way people could protect themselves better.

On February 26th, 2020, Elder Melo and I were riding our bikes, talking to people as we always did, when my phone started ringing. It was President Judd, and he said we had new instructions: Because of COVID, all missionaries in Japan would start quarantine. We bought enough food for the next two weeks and canceled Eikaiwa as well as our other appointments.

It was sad to be in quarantine, but I understood it was for our own protection. We could go to church to use the wi-fi and we used to have lessons with people we were teaching and other members. Through video, we started having many lessons every day. I set appointments with everyone we were teaching and tried to have spiritual messages with families from our ward. Technology was a great blessing during that moment.

President Judd also programmed meetings for us to teach each other and activities for the entire mission. Sister Judd even taught us new things to cook while we were in quarantine. President Judd also wanted us to help each other to be happy and optimistic during that uncertain moment and organized a way for us to minister to each other. Every night we needed to call another missionary, and someone would call us.

I had to call Elder Hull, who I knew, and Elder Jack called me. Elder Melo needed to call Elder McBride (who arrived in Japan with me) and Elder Monteiro called him. Later the designations changed. As a district leader, I also called the other missionaries in the district often.

Eventually, I talked with Elder Orsi, and he told me that he heard from someone that, if the mission was closed, all missionaries with less than 90 days left would finish their missions (not being reassigned to other places). He was very worried about that possible information and I was a little worried too, but I had faith that everything would work out in the end.

The bishop from Toyota called us and asked us to tell the people we were teaching that there wouldn't be sacrament meeting at church. I told him that I had already mentioned that to everyone and we were having lessons through "Line" and social media. I also asked to bishop to tell members that if they wanted us to participate in any family home evening (virtually) we would be happy to do so.

Everything was still uncertain, but the mission had changed a lot. Before we focused more on visiting people and going out and talking with absolutely anyone we saw, but now the work needed to be virtual. At that moment I saw that being companions with Elder Melo was a great blessing. Our days were still fun and optimistic, and we talked to one another all the time (since we were in quarantine), if I had a difficult companion, those days would've been hard, but they weren't.

The people from my district were also very nice and were trying their best to have a good attitude toward the new rules we had. Sister Mabalot was always happy, just like Elder Monteiro and Elder Moura. It was always nice to talk to them.

On March 12th, we received the news that the Coronavirus was now considered a pandemic. The following day, a sister from my district told me that she would go home the next day, because one of the islands from the Philippines would close all airports, and the church would send them home before it would be impossible for her to do so (she was already finishing her mission).

On March 15th, there was a baptism on the mission, from one of the family members of a family that I knew and had taught in Inuyama. The baptism had many rules for protection against COVID and very few people could attend, but the whole mission watched through "Zoom". It was a happy moment for all of us.

The next day, Elder Melo asked me to cut his hair. In my opinion, it was a bad idea, but he had the specific scissors to cut it and insisted that I try it. Since I usually laugh when I'm nervous, I laughed a lot while I was cutting his hair.

— Don't worry Irineu, it will be fine! – He said with a lot of courage while I was cutting it.

I did my best and didn't cut much on the front part, this way it wouldn't be very obvious that it was bad. It was the only time in my life that I cut someone's hair, and it wasn't as bad as I thought it would be, but I'm sure that anyone who understands more about hair would disagree.

On March 17th, my last transfer on the mission officially started, my 16th transfer. But on March 21st, President Judd sent us a message asking us to be present at a devotional at 10:00 am. I had a bad feeling.

We used Zoom to connect to the other missionaries in the mission and President Judd started speaking. He and Sister Judd were clearly very sad. He said that all the missionaries who were not native to Japan would go home and serve the rest of their missions in their own countries. Most of the missionaries in Nagoya were not native.

I was shocked by that revelation. I was on my last transfer, which meant I would just finish my mission, not be reassigned. But I had to trust the Lord and keep having faith.

25

Trapped in São Paulo

On March 24th, President Judd called us very early and told us that all missionaries of the mission had to go to the mission office as fast as we could because we would all go home. Elder Melo had helped me pack my bags the they before, so we were somewhat ready, but we still needed to finish packing some last things in our apartment.

I called many members of the church and asked if they could give us a ride to Nagoya, to the Meitou church building (which was right next to the mission office). Most of them couldn't. Then, the Matsumoto couple called us and said they were right next to our building waiting for us. Brother Suzuki had called them, and they were ready to help. I was very grateful.

Before leaving, I took a pill for motion sickness. Before my mission, I never got nauseated in a car, but during my mission, I had some problems with my stomach, so I usually took precautions before long travels.

We had a nice travel and arrived at Nagoya, where all the missionaries from the mission were gathering. I said goodbye to the Matsumoto family and thanked them for their help. President Judd had ordered pizza for us to have something for lunch.

Speaking of President Judd, he was very busy that day. He would receive calls from someone and would scream the name of one missionary or more, they had to leave and go to the airport, because their passage had been bought.

Later, in the afternoon, President Judd called all the Brazilian missionaries to his living room. As we arrived there, he explained that there was a problem. The airports in Brazil were closing, so the church would take us to São Paulo, but it could be very hard, or even impossible to get flights for our own states and cities. Of course, the Church would help us and pay for any expenses, but we had a decision to make: We could go and try to get home, or we could stay in Japan where the borders would close and we wouldn't be able to leave for many months (no one knew how many).

President Judd asked us to think about our choice and contact our families. I called my parents using Facebook Messenger and explained the situation. I only had a few weeks left on my mission, so it was better to go home than to be stuck in Japan for who knows how long, maybe even a year.

Elder Orsi was the first one to say that he would go home. His decision was a bit easier since he was from São Paulo, it would be easier for him to get home. Then, I told President Judd that I would go home as well.

The rest of the day was very stressful. I was waiting with over 46 other missionaries in the Meitou church building while President Judd received information about the plane tickets of random missionaries. Any moment it could be me, so I couldn't relax. My parents were also very nervous and kept sending me messages asking about the situation.

I wasn't the only one stressed. At one point, Elder Cavalcanti asked Elder Orsi and I for a priesthood comfort blessing. I had the honor to give him the blessing and even I felt better after that. President and Sister Judd asked for almost 100 burgers at McDonald's along with almost 100 fries and drinks for us to have what to have for dinner.

All the missionaries left would have to sleep close to the mission because the journey would continue on the next day. 31 Elders would sleep in the mission office and 15 Sisters would sleep on Gokiso, a close area that had room for everybody. In our attempt to calm down, Elder Orsi, Elder Melo, and I went for a walk around the mission office. Elder Orsi and I knew that place really well, so we wouldn't get lost.

At the end of the night, Elder Orsi and I sat next to President and Sister Judd, they were talking with many people and waiting for everyone's tickets. I don't think they slept at all that night. In the end, only Elder Monteiro and I had no flight passages.

My parents were very worried, as was I, but President Judd told me that he would not sleep until he had gotten me a flight passage. I thanked him a lot and felt that I needed to sleep, it was past midnight and the medicament for motion sickness always made me tired. Sister Judd told me where I could sleep, and I went to a room full of beds where four other missionaries were trying to sleep.

I lay down and tried to calm myself to sleep, even though I was so nervous about the next day. All the other Elders were whispering and talking to each other, but I really wanted to sleep, so I didn't say anything. They were talking about their missions and stories that they heard. Eventually, they mentioned the two Elders who got lost going to Okazaki.

— One of the Elders didn't have the "white mon", and the other one had – Someone said.

— I heard that it was Elder Irineu and some other missionary. Elder Irineu had the white mon – Another person said.

— The Elder Irineu who is in this room? – Someone asked.

— I think so.

— No, I heard it was… - And the person said other names.

I smiled. I didn't want to say it was Elder Wood who didn't have the "white mon", I also didn't want to spend a long time telling the whole story. It was funny how Elder Wood was right, and the story did become famous, but I was also right and no one knew it was him.

I barely slept, but woke up at 3:30 am to take a shower. Some other Elders were awake and I spent some time talking to them. I avoided telling my parents I was awake because I wanted to relax for a little while. It was even a little nostalgic to see Elder Orsi and Elder Cavalcanti there, at the same place where we had started our mission and spent our first night in Nagoya, back in 2018.

Eventually, I called President Judd and asked him if the church had been able to buy my ticket. And they had! I received the ticket and said goodbye to Elder Sherman, who would stay in Japan. Two members of the church took me, Elder Melo and Elder Farias to the airport.

I went to the counter with my luggage and showed my ticket on my tablet, but there was a mistake:

— Your passage does not exist for us – The woman said – I don't think you finished your purchase.

At that moment, I felt really desperate. What would I do? I couldn't even call President Judd and ask for help. I didn't have my phone anymore and had not memorized the mission office phone numbers.

Suddenly, I looked to my right and saw Sister Judd.

— Just a second – I asked the woman.

I ran toward Sister Judd and explained to her that people were saying that my passage didn't exist.

— Don't worry, we will fix this – She told me.

President Judd talked to the people at the airport and called someone who worked for the church. They talked for a while and I heard some parts of it.

— No, you have to decide now! – President Judd said firmly – The plane will leave soon and this Elder may stay trapped in Japan for indeterminate time! – He reminded the person.

I felt very nervous with this last part of the conversation. But apparently, the person had bought the ticket.

— President, I am so grateful you are here – I said with honesty.

— It's a miracle Elder Irineu. We would not come, but I felt that we should – He told me with a smile.

I will never forget that miracle or how much President Judd helped me. I am very grateful to him and to the Lord.

After that, I said goodbye to President and Sister Judd and entered my plane. There were many missionaries on that plane that I knew, including Elder Davis, Barton, Gluch, and Coelho.

We all parted ways in Tokyo, where Elder Coelho and I had lunch at MacDonald's (again) and boarded a plane toward England. There, we would take a plane to São Paulo. In the airplane, I was able to sleep a little bit, after all the flight was 12 hours long.

Elder Coelho and I arrived in London around 16:00, but our next flight would be only at 21:15, so we had to wait for some time. Unfortunately, everything was closed because of the pandemic and we couldn't change our money from yen to the right money. Because of that, we just waited for our flight. I was very grateful I wasn't alone on that travel.

At some point in the afternoon, I sneezed really loud and every single person in the airport looked at me.

— Irineu, at least cover your mouth – Elder Coelho whispered.

I laughed. The sneeze was so sudden that I didn't cover my mouth. But everyone was so afraid of COVID that sneezing was a bad idea at that moment. The night got really cold, but Elder Coelho had a spare coat in his bag and lent it to me.

But, now that things were more normal, I started to feel really sleepy, and I started to fall asleep while Elder Coelho was speaking.

— I'm sorry, Coelho, I woke up at 3:30 and didn't sleep well ever since – I explained.

— Yeah. I haven't slept since this morning – He agreed.

— When was this morning? – I asked.

— I have no idea – He said.

Days had become really confusing at that moment. It felt like I had been awake for over two days, but only now it was night. Of course, we had traveled half the world in the meantime, so it made since time was confusing now. I started to feel nauseated again, for some reason and took another pill for motion sickness that I had in my bag. That didn't help me to feel more awake.

I slept on the airplane before it took flight.

When I arrived at Guarulhos, in São Paulo, I saw many missionaries again. One of them was a great friend of mine (who lived in Porto Alegre) who had served in the Japan Fukuoka Mission, Elder Campos. He had been on the MTC with Elder Coelho, so they were friends.

In the airport, I also saw Elder Orsi (who soon went home), Elder Santos (who was in my district at the MTC), Cavalcanti, Correa, Monteiro, and others, including Sister Duarte, who was from Porto Alegre and served in the Japan Nagoya Mission with me. We would take the same flight home. Elder Melo was also there with his family and later went home with them.

I went to a counter with my passages (on my tablet).

— I'm sorry, but your flight was canceled – The woman told me.

— Cancelled? – I asked.

— Actually, they changed the date – She explained – Your flight will now be in May.

— In May?! – I asked. That was a month later – What am I going to do now?

— I'm sorry, I don't know – She said.

I left the counter and found a church employee who worked in the MTC and was there helping the missionaries. What had happened to me had happened to all the others arriving from Japan. I and all the missionaries who arrived from Japan gathered in a corner of the airport while the employee would take care of the problem.

The church, at that moment, was trying to take all the American missionaries out of Brazil. So, the airport was soon full of hundreds of missionaries from the church. There I met many Elders who had become friends in the MTC. It was fun to see all of those familiar friends from the beginning of my mission.

That afternoon I also met a Sister from Australia who was waiting for a flight to go home. But at that moment it was very difficult to get to Australia.

— Sister, have you ever heard about the "Great Emu War"? – I asked.

She closed her eyes for a second.

— Yes. How have you heard about it? – She asked me.

We both laughed and I explained how a companion of mine told me all about it. By the end of the night, all the American missionaries had left the airport. I lay on the floor and slept there a little bit.

— Irineu, don't lay on the floor! – Elder Cavalcanti told me – You could catch COVID!

— I don't think I care – I answered calmly. I was just too tired.

Eventually, a church employee took us, and many other missionaries to a bus. We arrived at a great hotel and I could sleep on a really nice bed. It was the first time I slept on a bed in almost two years. The next morning I ate breakfast at the hotel and felt heavenly.

Elder Coelho and Campus had lost their flight because the man who would drive them there (the same one who took me from the MTC and drove me to the airport) was late. That made the other church employees very angry, understandably.

We went back to the airport and, Elder Cavalcanti, Siter Duarte, and I were together for the whole day. There, an MTC employee helped us to do our check-in (we had the new tickets on our tablets) and told us where to wait for our flight. I was so grateful for his help and asked him if someone had asked him to help us. He said that he knew that there were missionaries at the airport needing help and he wanted to help.

What a great person.

The previous day we were able to switch our money from yen to reais. So, we bought a great lunch at the airport. A nice feijoada (rice with beans) and a steak. It was the best meal I had eaten in a few days.

At night, I said goodbye to Elder Cavalcanti, and we waited for our plane to Porto Alegre. There, I found another friend of mine. He was going to serve in the U.S.A., but he had asthma and needed to go home, to Porto Alegre.

— So, how would you describe your mission? – He asked me.

— It was miraculous – I answered – There were so many problems that I faced, even on the MTC, but the Lord blessed me, and everything worked out fine. The Lord blessed me so much and my mission was beautiful.

— That's amazing – He told me.

The three of us took a flight and went to Porto Alegre. The flight took less than 2 hours.

— It was so fast! – I said to Sister Duarte after the pilot said we were arriving.

— It was! – She said with a smile – This time we are not traveling to another country.

— True.

After many travels of over 10 hours, one hour and thirty minutes felt like nothing.

— Welcome to Porto Alegre – A voice said on the airplane.

I couldn't believe I was home. It felt like a dream coming to an end, and I had mixed feelings about it. Although I was very relieved to be home after all the stress of the last few days. My parents were at the airport, and I felt so happy to see them again. We all hugged for a few minutes. I sent a message to President Judd and told him that Sister Duarte and I had arrived at Porto Alegre. He thanked me.

Sometime later, my Stake President released me of my calling as a missionary. I felt a little sad and looked up. In his office, there were three big picture frames of the First Presidency: The prophet Russel

M. Nelson, President Oaks, and President Eyring. I saw their smiley faces and felt happy.

The Lord was happy with me, I could feel it. My mission had been indescribably good and was now finished.

Conclusion

Writing this book was a great and very personal experience. It was only possible because I wrote in my journal every single day of my mission, so the advice that I give to any person who asks me is "write in your journal every day".

My mission was a blessing to me and to other people and I am very grateful for everything that I lived during that time. The Lord placed many angels on my pathway, and they all helped me on my journey. I think that's how life works. It's just more noticeable during the mission.

During my mission, I met many missionaries who would quote a scripture at the end of their missions: "I have fought a good fight, I have finished my course, I have kept the faith" (2 Timothy 4:7). However, I never thought it was very appropriate using that scripture at the end of our missions. The Apostle Paul said that at the end of his life, and I think that is the real meaning of the scripture.

The mission is not the end of our lives, just like accepting baptism is not the end, but the beginning. After our missions, we still need to keep our faith, be faithful to our covenants, and help others. After our mission's end, we still need to be vigilant, pray always, and read the scriptures. We need to seek the Lord's Spirit every day and ask for his guidance.

And I know He will guide us. He is always by our side.

Daniel Franca Irineu was born in Rio Grande do Sul, in the South of Brazil. From a young age, he always enjoyed reading different literary genres by different authors.

From a Young age he wrote stories full of adventures and fantasies. He has published the books of fiction and fantasy, among them the book "Entre Sonhos e Batalhas" and the saga "As Pedras do Apocalipse".

Milton Keynes UK
Ingram Content Group UK Ltd.
UKHW020827141124
451205UK00012B/761